The NEW TESTAMENT

The NEW TESTAMENT

The Good News of Jesus

Michael Pennock

Ave Maria Press • Notre Dame, Ind. 46556

Nihil Obstat:

Rev. Paul J. Hritz, S.T.L.
Censor Deputatus

Imprimatur:

Most Rev. Anthony M. Pilla, D.D., M.A.
Bishop of Cleveland

Library of Congress Catalog Card Number: 82-70088
International Standard Book Number: 0-87793-246-8

Photography:

Joseph De Caro, 32, 40; Paul Conklin, 66, 226; Rev. J. Murray Elwood, cover, 82, 85, 113, 132, 138, 148, 156, 175, 184, 248; John E. Fitzgerald, 120, 166; Robert Maust, 74; Rick Smolan, 20, 206; Justin Soleta, 104; Russell A. Thompson, 196; Paul Tucker, 236; Jim Whitmer, 97; Betty Hurwich-Zoss, 46, 216.

Art: Betsy French

Manufactured in the United States of America.

DEDICATION

For my wife Carol whose love for me and our children, Scott, Jennifer, Amy and Christopher, makes the good news of the Lord come alive for all of us.

Acknowledgments

First, I would like to thank my immediate family for all the loving support they give to my vocation of catechist.

Next, I wish to thank my editor at Ave Maria Press—Frank Cunningham. He is a source of great encouragement to me. Ave's associate editor, Joan Bellina, has helped me make this a better book. She also deserves my gratitude. I also wish to acknowledge Gene Geissler of Ave Maria and Charles Jones. All these people help make the lonely task of writing a great source of fulfillment.

I have been most fortunate to study Scripture under some eminent scholars in years past. Fr. Gene LaVerdiere and Fr. Carroll Stuhlmueller have given me some deep insights into the Lord's word. The eminent New Testament scholar Joachim Jeremias has enflamed me with a love of God's word that can never die. My friend and mentor, Fr. Paul Hritz, has shared with me the valuable lesson of helping people see how God's word lives today. I thank the Lord for all of them.

My friends Mary Jane Treichel and Mary Lou Salzano read the first draft with critical eyes. Their many suggestions have helped me immensely.

I also wish to thank once again some of my teachers who have helped me in my ministry: Fr. Mark DiNardo, Dr. George Eppley and Dr. Steve Thompson.

I am proud to be a member of the faculty of St. Ignatius High School, Cleveland, Ohio. The Jesuits there have supported my work over the past 12 years. My colleagues in the theology department have both inspired and encouraged me. Thanks to Fr. Ron Torina, S.J., Fr. Larry Belt, S.J., Jim Skerl, Marty Dybicz, Paul Rodgers, S.J., Sr. Carolyn Capuano, H.M., Mary Lou Salzano and Tom Healey.

The Lord has presented himself to me time and again through my students: adults who attend parish series, college undergraduates, colleagues who are enrolled in graduate courses and, especially, my students at St. Ignatius High School. In fact, my students, who show me that the Lord's word is a living word, are my greatest source of inspiration. I am especially grateful for the many young men I have been privileged to teach at St. Ignatius and for their parents who are concerned with their spiritual welfare. Many of these students have entered my classroom as strangers; I can honestly say, though, that many of them leave as true friends in the Lord. I wish to thank here especially John Reilly, Ken Gulick, Tom Jordan and Mark Johnson who helped me with this book.

Thanks, too, to Darrell Dell'Andrea who typed my manuscript.

To all of these people and to others who have supported and encouraged me, may God bless you.

—Michael Francis Pennock

Contents

1

Background for Reading the New Testament: What Is the New Testament?

Ignorance of the scriptures is ignorance of Christ.

—St. Jerome

Christians and Jews believe that the Bible is God's word, a word that still lives today. Is the Bible, though, just another word which is competing for your attention? Consider the many words today that affect you:

- Advertising entices you to buy products that will help make you look handsome or beautiful or get people to think well of you.
- Rock songs sing their message of love and love lost.
- Newspapers inform you of the current troubles in the world.
- Movies and TV programs delight, intrigue or frighten you with stories of passion, mystery and horror.
- School books offer you the information you will need to get into college or further some kind of career after high school.

All the words used by these various media compete for your attention. They all want you to think they are important. Christians, however, firmly believe that their scriptures are the most important of all because they contain the words of salvation, the good news of God's friendship with humanity in our Lord Jesus Christ.

Our study of God's word will focus on part of The Book (*Bible* means "book"), namely, the New Testament. The New *Testament* refers to the new *covenant* of friendship won for us by Jesus Christ. It is the record of the incredible good news that we are loved by God and that we have a destiny of eternal life in union with him. This good news is as good today as it was almost 2,000 years ago when a man by the name of Jesus from Nazareth walked the earth. It is his message come alive today. By reading the New Testament we can hear for ourselves the word of God that gives life. This word—the word of God recorded for all time—proclaims the best possible news you could ever hear: God loves you!

Before beginning our study of the New Testament, test your knowledge of God's book by taking this short quiz. Check the answers on page 14 to see how much you already know.

SHORT QUIZ ON THE NEW TESTAMENT

1. ____ There are ? books in the New Testament. a. 23; b. 45; c. 27; d. 18; e. 35.
2. ____ The earliest gospel written was a. Matthew; b. Mark; c. Luke; d. John.
3. ____ The gospels were originally written in which language? a. Greek; b. Aramaic; c. Latin; d. Hebrew.
4. ____ The New Testament was composed immediately after the death and resurrection of Jesus. (True or False)
5. ____ Who wrote the Acts of the Apostles? a. John; b. Luke; c. Peter; d. Paul.
6. ____ Each of the gospel authors wrote for different communities in the early church. (True or False)
7. ____ Which of these New Testament books is the shortest? a. The gospel of Mark; b. 1 Thessalonians; c. 3 John; d. Philemon.
8. ____ The most difficult book of the New Testament to understand and the one with the most symbolism is a. Revelation; b. Romans; c. gospel of John; d. 2 Corinthians; e. 1 Peter.
9. ____ The canon of the New Testament refers to the official list of New Testament books. (True or False)
10. ____ The core teaching, the proclamation of Jesus as Lord, is known by the technical term a. didache; b. koinonia; c. kerygma; d. diakonia.

11. ____ In all cases, the gospels give *identical* accounts of the life of Jesus. (True or False)

12. ____ A book that will help you find any word that is used in the Bible is called a a. dictionary of the Bible; b. lexicon; c. commentary; d. concordance.

13. ____ The New American Bible is a fine Catholic *translation* of the Bible into English. (True or False)

14. ____ __?__ refers to studying how the New Testament authors *edited* their sources in writing their works. a. redaction criticism; b. form criticism; c. source criticism; d. hermeneutics.

15. ____ In general, *inspiration* refers to the divine origin of the Bible. (True or False)

How did you do on the quiz? Do you know more than you thought you knew? St. Jerome said that not to know the Bible is to be ignorant of Christ. Jerome, who translated the Bible into Latin in the fourth and fifth centuries, spoke for many Christians when he made his wise observation. We *meet* Jesus in the New Testament. Our Lord is truly present in his scriptural word. Spend time reading the New Testament and you will be rewarded with an experience of meeting the Lord. His word will help you live a better life. His word will help you discover what is really important. May God be with you on your journey through the New Testament.

The first chapter will help you learn more about the Bible by looking at the following topics:

- the earliest proclamation about Jesus
- how the New Testament came about: the historical Jesus, oral tradition, the writings
- an overview of the books of the New Testament
- how scholars study the New Testament
- some key information about the New Testament

The chapter will conclude with a summary and some exercises. Throughout the book there will be a number of reading exercises for you to do so that you can hear God's word for yourself. Please try to do all of these as you proceed in your study.

THE BEGINNING: WHAT WAS PREACHED ABOUT JESUS

Imagine a group of frightened people, confused and uncertain, huddled somewhere in a house in Jerusalem. Three days before, their leader, Jesus of Nazareth, had been unmercifully scourged and crucified by the Roman authorities. He died. Their faith in him as the Messiah had been dashed.

But on Easter Sunday this same Jesus appeared to them—the apostles and some other disciples. He revealed himself as one alive, one who had been raised up by his Father. This Jesus, the Messiah who is both Lord and Son of God, made a number of appearances. Forty days later, according to Luke's account, Jesus ascended to heaven. There he sits in glory with his Father.

While Jesus was with his disciples during his earthly ministry, he promised that he would send his Spirit to comfort and guide them. Luke tells us that the Holy Spirit came upon the apostles on *Pentecost* Sunday. Pentecost was a major Jewish feast which celebrated the harvest and commemorated Moses' reception of the Law on Mt. Sinai. It took place 50 days after the Jewish feast of Passover. On this day the Holy Spirit came in power. Immediately the apostles began preaching the good news of salvation to the Jews who were gathered in Jerusalem for the festival. Acts records Peter's testimony about Jesus given on that important Pentecost Sunday. It gives us an important glimpse of what the early Christians preached from the very beginning. Pause here and see for yourself what Peter said.

Read Acts 2.

What an incredible talk Peter gave on that first Pentecost, the day Christians celebrate as the birthday of the church. Here's an outline of that first sermon, a talk so moving that it resulted in the conversion of 3,000 people.

1. Peter reassures his audience that the apostles are not drunk. (After all, it is still only 9 a.m.!) What people are eye- and ear-witnessing is the fulfillment of a

prophecy made to Joel (see Jl 3:1-5) as to what will happen when the Lord sends his Spirit. In fact, Peter is announcing that the messianic age has come!

2. Peter reviews the marvelous deeds that Jesus performed when he was in their midst.
3. Peter tells how Jesus was put to death by the Jews in cooperation with the Romans (that is, "men outside the Law").
4. He reports that Jesus has been raised from the dead and is exalted with the Father as it had been prophesied in one of the psalms (16:8-11).
5. He reaffirms that the Holy Spirit has come in power.
6. What is left, Peter concludes, is for his audience to repent, be baptized in the name of Jesus Christ for the forgiveness of sin, and receive the Holy Spirit.

These six points give us a good idea of what early Christians like Peter and Paul had to say about Jesus. They contain the *kerygma,* that is, the essential good news about Jesus Christ. This core teaching about Jesus was aimed at converting the Jews and later the Gentiles (non-Jews). It showed how the Old Testament prophecies applied to Jesus. It recounted Jesus' life, his teaching and miracles. It told about his death by crucifixion. Most important, this preaching witnessed to our Lord's resurrection and the gift of the Holy Spirit who has been poured out on anyone who believes in Jesus.

When Peter preached the good news he expected people to respond in *faith.* The message is the same today. We should repent by turning from sin. We should accept baptism and receive the gift of the Holy Spirit.

Many sermons like Peter's were preached in the early church before anything was written down. Luke, who wrote Acts between A.D. 80 and 90, records several of these sermons. A reflection on these sermons gives us an idea of how the writings came to be. First, Jesus lived his earthly life. Then, the apostles preached the good news of his resurrection and the incredible news of God's love for us in Jesus. Finally, after some time went by, they committed the good news to writing. The examples used in the following chart show how this took place.

GROWTH OF THE NEW TESTAMENT

TIME LINE		*STAGES*
Birth of Jesus—	4-6 B.C.	Stage 1: *The historical Jesus* events of Jesus' life, death and resurrection
Death of Jesus—	A.D. 30	Stage 2: *Oral tradition* preaching in faith about Jesus; emergence of Christian communities in Israel and throughout the Gentile world.
1 Thessalonians—	A.D. 51	Stage 3: *New Testament writings* 1. *Paul's letters* to new Christian congregations (death of the apostles; end of the world does *not* take place; new converts need proper instruction)
Gospel of Mark—	A.D. 70	2. *Written gospels* (problems relating to Gentile culture; rising heresies; need to organize and nurture the ever-growing communities)
Revelation—	A.D. 90-100	3. *Other "apostolic" writings and the book of Revelation* (spread of martyrdom; persecutions under Domitian—A.D. 96; some Christians abandon their faith)

Answers to quiz on page 10

1. c	6. True	11. False
2. b	7. c	12. d
3. a	8. a	13. True
4. False	9. True	14. a
5. b	10. c	15. True

READING EXERCISES

A. *Kerygmatic sermons:* Read one of the following sermons preached by Peter or Paul and outline its content. How is this sermon similar to the sermon you just studied (Acts 2)? How is it different?

Sermons

- Peter to the Jews (Acts 3:11-26)
- Peter to the Sanhedrin (Acts 4:1-12)
- Peter to the Gentiles (Acts 10:34-43)
- Paul to the Jews (Acts 13:14-43)

Brief Outline

____

____

____

____

____

____

Now read Paul's speech in Acts 17:22-34. Answer these two questions:

a. What major differences do you notice between this speech to the Gentiles at Athens and the other kerygmatic sermons?

____

____

b. How might you explain the differences? ______________

____

____

B. Part of the early preaching about Jesus attempted to show how certain prophecies from the Hebrew scriptures applied to him. Here are some of these famous prophecies. Read two of them. Briefly summarize what they are promising. Then briefly state how these prophecies applied to Jesus.

Prophecies	**Summary and application**
Isaiah 11 (Description of the Messiah)	
Isaiah 52:13-53 (Suffering Servant of God)	
Ezekiel 34 (Promise of the Good Shepherd)	
Daniel 7 (Vision of the Son of Man)	

Also read Hosea 6:2.
What does it prophesy?

Stage 1: The Historical Jesus

All the New Testament writings are ultimately based on the existence of a man who was known in his lifetime as Jesus from Nazareth; Jesus the Carpenter; or Jesus, the son of Joseph (Mark's gospel calls him the son of Mary). During the past 100 years or so, scholars have penetrated the gospels and other New Testament writings in a quest for the historical Jesus. Behind the writings they see a man who was born in Bethlehem between 4 and 6 B.C.* in the reign of Herod the Great. They seem to agree that Jesus began his teaching ministry around A.D. 28 and that he died on Friday, April 7, in the year 30.

This Jesus of history was one of us. Like us, he knew fatigue, hunger, loneliness and disappointments. Like us, he learned new things.

Jesus was a teacher. He taught his message in synagogues and in open fields and on lake shores. He gathered around him a dozen men from various walks of life. Women and children, tax collectors and sinners, even the famous followed him.

People also knew Jesus as a prophet, a spokesman for God—but a prophet who was rejected in his own hometown of Nazareth (Lk 4:24). Jesus claimed unique authority in his teaching about the Father. This claim was brought out forcefully in the Sermon on the Mount in such phrases as "You have learned how it was said to our ancestors . . . but I say this to you" (Mt 5:21-22). His use of "Amen" to begin his sayings contrasted sharply with the normal custom of the Jews. They ended their prayers to God with "Amen" as a sign of hope that God would act on their prayers; Jesus used it his way to show a unique relationship with God.

What did he teach? He proclaimed God's kingdom as a present reality. He performed many miracles and signs to underscore that teaching. He cured lepers, gave sight to the blind and hearing to the

* In 525 a Roman monk named Dionysius Exiguus (Denis the Little—of size, not intellect!) redated the existing Roman calendar to coincide with the birth of Jesus Christ. Events that took place before Jesus' birth were dated B.C.; events after his birth were dated A.D. It was discovered some centuries afterward that Dionysius miscalculated Jesus' birth which had to precede Herod's death in 4 B.C. (see Mt 2:19).

deaf. He fed the multitudes. He helped the lame to walk. He drove demons out of the possessed. He did these things to show that God's kingdom had broken into human history, that a new age of peace and justice and reconciliation had begun. He also preached that God's kingdom had a future aspect that awaits final fulfillment.

As part of his preaching the kingdom Jesus called for repentance, a complete turning away from sin. He commanded faith in the gospel. He saw people as either for him or against him. In addition Jesus professed to forgive sin. Unlike other prophets he stepped in to heal the breach sinners had made when they broke their relationship with God and others. To highlight this claim to unique authority before God and his fellow humans, Jesus did what no self-respecting Jew would dare do: He befriended sinners, prostitutes, tax collectors.

His teaching took the form of parables. In the famous story of the Prodigal Son, he taught about his Father's great love for sinners. In the story of the Good Samaritan he taught that all people, even our enemies, deserve our respect and love. These and many other parables characterized Jesus' teaching and helped his disciples remember his message of God's incredible love for his children. Jesus lived in an age not of books but of memory and the living voice of teachers. He gave his teaching a unique stamp adapted to his hearers. His chosen apostles saw him perform his deeds and heard his words and consequently were able later to witness to him under the guidance of the Holy Spirit.

Above all else, though, Jesus came as one who dared to claim a one-of-a-kind, personal relationship with the God of the Jews. He called God "Abba" which is similar to our word *daddy* (see Mk 14:36). This address connotes an intimacy without parallel in the Judaism of his time. Jesus' whole outlook was centered on doing his Father's will and on preaching his kingdom. He invited all his followers to address the almighty God with the same intimacy, "Our Father." He challenged his hearers to respond to his Father's will and to follow his own example of love.

The rest of Jesus' story is quite familiar to you. His message and his deeds brought him in opposition to the religious leaders of the day. He said his authority was greater than that of Moses. He claimed to forgive sin, associated with outcasts, promised salvation and criticized the complacency of the official leaders. Because Jesus did these things, he was accused of a kind of blasphemy whereby he appeared to assume certain privileges which were God's alone. "But that only made the Jews even more intent on killing him, because, not content with breaking the sabbath, he spoke of God as his own Father, and so made himself God's equal" (Jn 5:18).

Things reached a boiling point when Jesus drove out those who were buying and selling in the Temple area. "This came to the ears of the chief priests and the scribes, and they tried to find some way of doing away with him; they were afraid of him because the people were carried away by his teaching" (Mk 11:18). Jesus did not flee from the plan to arrest him. He did not claim any kind of political power and, in fact, warned his disciples that those who use the sword will perish by it. He was tried under Jewish law and then turned over to the Romans where he was again tried, scourged and crucified. At his Last Supper with the disciples he foretold his impending death and said that it was a death for the remission of sins.

His death on a cross meant failure and disillusionment for his disciples. Their faith was shattered. Their hopes crumpled to the ground. They were at a loss.

But then there was the resurrection!

SOME THINGS TO DO

A. *Searching for the historical Jesus.* Scholars agree that there is very little evidence for the existence of Jesus outside of the New Testament. But there is some. Roman historians by the names of Suetonius, Tacitus and Pliny the Younger do mention something about Jesus and his followers. So, too, does the famous Jewish historian Josephus. Check a resource like John L. McKenzie's *Dictionary of the Bible* (New York: The Macmillan Company, 1965) under the heading "Jesus Christ" to see what these men said about Jesus. Many other books on Jesus give an account of these nonbiblical sources, too. Share your findings with the class.

B. *Who is Jesus Christ?* Here is a list of 11 statements about Jesus. Christians would accept all of them as true. Nonbelievers would not accept them all. Check off those statements which a non-Christian would have problems accepting as true about Jesus. Then discuss why this would be so.

Statements

1. Jesus ate with sinners. ______
2. Jesus numbered women among his friends. ______
3. Jesus is the Messiah (the Christ). ______
4. Jesus' headquarters were in Capernaum. ______

5. Jesus is Lord ______
6. Jesus Christ is alive today and can be received in the Eucharist. ______
7. Pontius Pilate put Jesus to death. ______
8. Jesus saved us. ______
9. Jesus often preached against phoniness. ______
10. Jesus knew he was especially chosen by God. ______
11. Jesus is present to us in the gospels. ______

C. *Jesus, significant people and you.* Skim through one of the gospels and make a list of the five most significant people Jesus met; that is, people who meant a lot to him. Give a reference and also list a key quality of the person. In another column list the five most significant people in your life and give their outstanding quality.

Jesus' Life

	person	reference	quality
1.	______	______	______
2.	______	______	______
3.	______	______	______
4.	______	______	______
5.	______	______	______

Your Life

	person	quality
1.	______	______
2.	______	______
3.	______	______
4.	______	______
5.	______	______

Discuss:

a. Share your choices. Why did you choose as you did? What made these people important for Jesus? Why are the people you listed important to you?

b. Is there any similarity between the people who were significant in Jesus' life and the people who are significant in your life? Explain.

Stage 2: Oral Tradition

Imagine your reaction if you were an early disciple of Jesus living in Palestine in the first century and the dead Jesus appeared to you as one alive. You would probably be bursting with joy and enthusiasm. Furthermore, empowered with the Holy Spirit, you would hardly be able to contain your overwhelming joy. You would absolutely have to share the good news of Jesus Christ with others.

This is exactly how the early church reacted to the good news of Jesus Christ. In an initial burst of enthusiasm early Christians went around the Holy Land and throughout the Roman Empire to preach the good news of salvation in Jesus Christ. They shared the message in Greece and Egypt, in Asia Minor and Syria, even in Rome itself. The preaching basically took three forms in this period:

1. The *kerygma*, or preaching to unbelievers. We have already seen some famous examples of this in the kerygmatic sermons of Paul and Peter. To aid in this preaching, the apostles and other disciples probably would have had in mind the basic outline or skeleton of Jesus' works, his death, resurrection and ascension. They would have had relevant Old Testament passages before them to help in showing how the prophecies made about the Messiah were fulfilled in Jesus.

2. The *didache,* or further catechetical instructions for those who accepted the good news. Early Christians who had just accepted the gospel hungered for more knowledge of what it meant to live a Christ-filled life. Lists of sayings of Jesus that might have been used for this deeper instruction were collected. One famous example is the Sermon on the Mount (Mt 5-7), a collection of Jesus' sayings on how his followers should live.

3. The *liturgy,* or the worship of the Christians. The way people pray reflects the way they believe. Certain key events, teachings and prayers were recalled in the early eucharistic celebrations. Some examples are the words of institution of the Eucharist Jesus used at the Last Supper, the Lord's

> Prayer, and the story of the passion of Jesus. In some cases the different communities would have slight variations in the wording, but the spirit of what Jesus said and did was recounted in all of the assemblies. For example, the wording of the Our Father differed slightly from community to community. We can see this even today when we read the gospels of Luke (11:2-4) and Matthew (6:9-13).

The material that was saved and passed on was shaped by the different communities. The early Christians were not so much interested in preserving an exact biography of Jesus as in interpreting the meaning of key events, deeds and sayings of Jesus. They filtered out unnecessary details and saved the heart of the message, adapting it to the audiences who heard it and relating it to the Old Testament background.

Several reasons prompted the early Christians to move from this stage of oral tradition to the third stage, the stage of the written New Testament. First, Jesus did not return when they expected him to do so. Because of some things Jesus had said during his earthly ministry, many early Christians thought wrongly that the end of the world would come in their lifetime. So they did not bother to write down anything about the good news. Why should they? There were more important things to do—preach the good news and get ready for Jesus' return. But they were wrong about the end. Eyewitnesses were dying. It became necessary to preserve an accurate account of what was preached.

A second reason for writing down the good news was to offer more instruction to new converts. Communities converted by Paul, who traveled from one end of the Roman Empire to another, always were in need of further instruction and sometimes for correction to help them maintain proper belief.

Finally, some writings and teachings appeared which did not reflect what the apostles witnessed about Jesus. To counteract these writings and teachings and to preserve the essence of the good news, it became necessary to commit the oral preaching to writing.

TWO THOUGHT PROVOKERS

1. a. Read Philippians 2:6-11.

   b. Summarize it here: ______

   c. This passage from Philippians was at first part of the oral tradition. Circle the kind of oral tradition you believe it was.

   (1) kerygma (2) didache (3) part of the liturgy

   Why did you choose as you did? ______

2. You might recall that the term *didache* refers to the further teaching new converts received after baptism. As mentioned above, the Sermon on the Mount is a good example of teaching that applies to all Christians, even today. Please read a short part of that sermon, Matthew 7:1-5. Then, outline a three-point talk directed to a group of your classmates. Present the teaching in a way that would be meaningful at your school today. Share your talk with at least one other classmate.

   a. ______

   b. ______

   c. ______

Stage 3: New Testament Writings

Finally, we have the writings themselves. These writings include the four gospels, letters written to various Christian communities, a chronicle of the early church (Acts) and a highly symbolic work known as Revelation.

One of the important things to note is how different authors recorded the same basic material. Each adopted the oral tradition in his own unique way for the community he was addressing. For example, both Luke and Matthew followed the same basic outline in writing their gospels: Jesus' baptism; his career in Galilee; his trip to Jerusalem; his passion, death and resurrection. But they arranged their material differently, and each emphasized certain things that the other did not. Why? Simply because they were writing for different communities with their own particular problems and interests. For example, Luke wrote for a non-Jewish (Gentile) Christian audience. He was trying to stress that Jesus was the Lord who came to save *all* men and women, Jew and Gentile alike, the poor as well as the rich, the outcast as well as the socially comfortable. Matthew, in contrast, wrote for a group of Christians who had been Jews. He was more concerned to show that Jesus fulfilled all the promises made to the Jews, that he was the fulfillment of the Jewish religion.

Luke and Matthew used their editorial skills to emphasize their overriding theme. In other words, they adapted their material to fit their audience.

To see this for yourself, read and compare the following passages on prayer:

Mt 6:5-15

Lk 11:1-14

Did you notice any differences in the two didaches (teachings) on how to pray?

We might outline the two readings on prayer like this:

MATTHEW	LUKE
1. When you pray	1. Jesus himself prayed
2. Don't be phony	2. Show us how to pray
3. Don't babble on; keep prayers short	3. Here's a formula: Our Father
4. Here's an example of a short prayer: Our Father	4. Parable of friend: Be persistent
5. Have forgiveness in in your heart	5. Parable of father: Your prayer will be answered

These are certainly different teachings on prayer; in fact, even the versions of the Our Father are a bit different. How can we explain this phenomenon? If we remember that Matthew and Luke were writing for diverse communities, the differences make more sense.

As mentioned before, Matthew wrote for Jewish Christians. He assumed that these Jewish converts *did* pray because Jews had a rich heritage of prayer. His gospel instructs the followers of Jesus to keep their prayers short and to the point (as in the Our Father). They should trust that God will answer their prayers, prayers that ask for God's will to be done. And Christians should pray with forgiveness in their hearts. Matthew cautions his audience *not* to pray as hypocrites do—showing off so that others will think they are holy. This teaching on prayer would make a lot of sense to a converted Jew who had accepted Jesus.

Luke, on the other hand, wrote for Gentile converts. They had been pagans who did not normally pray. In his teaching Luke points out that Jesus himself prayed (a Jew would have known this). Luke tells his audience that Jesus taught the perfect prayer, the Our Father. In this prayer, the Christian can call God "Abba" (Father). Luke is stressing that the Christian God is loving and deeply concerned with his children. Pagans did not know this. Their gods were often cruel and worked against people. In addition Luke underscores the need for persistence in prayer. Finally he assures the community that its prayers will be answered. (His Gentile-Christian audience needed these reminders because Gentiles did not have the Jewish experience of praying with trust that God would answer prayers.)

Other examples of how New Testament authors work with the oral tradition will be given when you study the four gospels.

TO THINK ABOUT AND TO DO

A. *You and prayer.* Let us look further into prayer now that we have studied what Jesus taught about it. Answer questions 1-8 with a *yes* or a *no*; questions 9-13 with a word or a brief phrase.

1. Do you normally "show off" when you pray? ____
2. Do you rarely pray? ____
3. If you pray, do your prayers drag on and on? ____
4. Do you get easily discouraged when you pray? ____
5. Is the Our Father one of your least favorite prayers? ____
6. Do you need encouragement to pray often? ____
7. Do you tend to hold grudges? ____
8. Do you often doubt that your prayers will be answered? ____

9. Does Luke's or Matthew's teaching on prayer make more sense to you?

____

10. How do you define prayer? ________________________

____

11. When do you pray?__________ Where?______________

12. Do you think it is important to pray? Why or why not?

____

13. When has prayer helped you? ____________________

____

*How did you answer the short survey above? If you answered yes to questions 2, 4, 6 and 8, Luke's didache on prayer is probably meant for you. If you answered yes to questions 1, 3, 5 and 7, you can grow in your prayer life by reflecting on the reading from Matthew.

Discussion: Share responses to question 10. As a class, choose the best definition.

Reflection: Questions 9, 11, 12 and 13 are for your own reflection. You may want to share your responses with a friend.

B. *Another example from Luke and Matthew.* Here is a fun exercise in biblical analysis to see if you can apply what you learned in this section of the chapter. Remember that Luke wrote for a Gentile-Christian audience and that Matthew wrote for a Jewish-Christian audience.

Jesus' family tree. Read Luke 3:23-38 and Matthew 1:1-16. Then answer these questions:

1. Were Luke and Matthew concerned to give an exact historical record of Jesus' ancestry? Why or why not?

____

____

2. To which man does Luke trace Jesus' ancestry?__________

To which man does Matthew trace Jesus' ancestry? ________

3. Can you think of a possible theological reason which can explain the difference you discovered in question 2?

____

____

OVERVIEW OF THE WRITINGS

Before listing the New Testament books, a word about the New Testament *canon* and about *inspiration* is in order. The Greek word *kanon* originally meant "measuring rod"; later it came to mean "rule" or "norm." The New Testament canon refers to the official list of 27 books which the church considers inspired, books that serve as the "rule" of faith and morals.

The history of the development of the New Testament canon is fascinating. St. Athanasius—a Father of the church—fixed the canon at 27 books in the year 367. The Council of Trent (1545-1563) taught as a matter of church doctrine that this list was the inspired word of God left with the church. New Testament writings were included in the canon because they reflected the faith of Christians, they were widely circulated in the early church, and they were based on the witness of the apostles.

The issue of the canon is related to inspiration. The noted Catholic scripture scholar Wilfrid Harrington, O.P., put it this way: "The books are inspired because God is their author; they are canonical because the church has recognized them and acknowledged them to be inspired." *Inspiration* means that God is the author of the Bible without in any way denying the free and personal activity of the human writer. Vatican II taught:

> In composing the sacred books, God chose men and while employed by Him they made use of their powers and abilities, so that with Him acting in them and through them, they, as true authors, consigned to writing everything and only those things which He wanted (*Constitution on Divine Revelation,* No. 11).

The following chart lists the New Testament canon according to types of writing, books, dates and authorship. In many cases scholars can only approximate the dates and the authorship of the given books. A very short summary or highlight for each writing is provided.

NEW TESTAMENT WRITINGS

	Book	Date	Author	Content
Gospels & Acts	Matthew	70-90	Jewish convert to Christianity	Jesus = Messiah and Lawgiver
	Mark	65-70	disciple of Peter	Jesus Christ = Suffering Servant
	Luke	70-90	Gentile convert to Christianity	Jesus Christ = Universal Messiah
	Acts	"	"	sequel to gospel of Luke; Spirit-led church spreads from Jerusalem to Rome
	John	90-100	possibly a disciple of John the apostle	Jesus = Son of God and Word of God
Paul's Letters	1 Thessalonians	51	Paul	Christians who already died will share in the Lord's Second Coming
	2 Thessalonians	51	Paul or perhaps his disciple	world is not to end yet; continue to work
	Galatians	54-57	Paul	Gentile converts don't have to follow Jewish laws and customs
	1 Corinthians	55-57	Paul	practical problems such as the Eucharist and resurrection treated
	2 Corinthians	55-57	Paul	defense of Paul's apostleship and authority against false teachers
	Romans	56-58	Paul	an introduction of Paul and his message; many consider this his greatest letter
	Philippians	56-63	Paul	thanks them for aid and reviews his teaching

	Philemon	61-63	Paul	sent from prison about a runaway slave who is equal to his master in faith
	Colossians	61-63	Paul or perhaps his disciple	attack on false teachers who tried to pervert Christianity
	Ephesians	61-63?	Paul or one of his students	church as one body of Christ
	1 Timothy 2 Timothy Titus	65-67? or more probable, 100-110?	Paul or, more probable, one of his later followers	these three letters are called the Pastoral Letters and deal with church order, organization, doctrine—institutional matters
Other "Apostolic" Writings & Revelation	1 Peter	64	?, perhaps Peter	to encourage persecuted Christians in Asia Minor
	James	62 or 80s	?	written about the moral life; mentions confession and anointing of the sick
	Jude	70s-90s	?, "Jude"	warns strongly against false teachers
	1 John 2 John 3 John	90s-110	disciple of John	these reiterate the teaching on love found in John's gospel and warn against false teachers
	2 Peter	100-110	?	urges Christians to grow in faith; warns against false teachers
	Hebrews	80-90	?	an elegant sermon written to bolster faith; teaches that Jesus is High Priest
	Revelation	90-100	a prophet named John	seven letters addressed to different churches; encourages persecuted Christians to be faithful even to death; lots of symbolism

TO DO

1. List at least three different kinds of writings in the New Testament. ______________________

   ____

2. Note the time span between the resurrection and the various writings.

   ____

3. How does the list above differ from the listing in your New Testament? ______________________

4. Check your New Testament and find the answers to these questions:
   a. Which is the longest gospel? ______________________
   b. Which is the shortest gospel? ______________________
   c. Which is Paul's longest letter? ______________________

HOW SCHOLARS STUDY THE NEW TESTAMENT

The New Testament is the most studied book in the world. Over the past 100 years or so, scholars have developed certain approaches for studying the New Testament. These approaches are commonly accepted methods of research today. Some of the most important ones are briefly described here.

Historical criticism

This method of study attempts to answer the question: What really took place behind the particular biblical text which is being studied? For example, you might note that Matthew reports that Pilate posted a guard at the tomb of Jesus after he was buried (Mt 27:62-66). None of the other gospel writers reports this event. Historical criticism asks the question: What really happened?

Source criticism

This technique tries to discover what materials the authors had in front of them when they wrote their own works. For example, read the following three passages which discuss Jesus' saying about salt: Matthew 5:13, Mark 9:49-50, and Luke 14:34-35. Noticing these and many other similar expressions shared among these three gospel writers, scholars have concluded that Matthew and Luke both had the gospel of Mark as one of their sources.

Form criticism

This type of analysis focuses on the small units found in the New Testament writings rather than on the whole documents. It tries to determine how these forms took shape in the period of the church's oral tradition before anything was written down. Some of the literary forms are proverbs, parables, pronouncement stories and miracle stories.

Redaction criticism

You have already done a little bit of redaction criticism in the discussion of how Matthew and Luke arranged their particular teaching on prayer (see pages 25-26) and in the exercise on page 27. Redaction criticism studies the history of the oral transmission of the particular text with the goal of discovering the theological perspectives of the particular writer. This is done by analyzing how he edited and composed his material. Redaction criticism is also interested in identifying how a particular writer through his individual style helped serve the community for which he wrote.

Hermeneutics

This is also called the science of bible meaning. It tries to show what a particular author had in mind when he wrote a passage. It also helps a person to discover how to give the sense of a scripture passage to others. A priest, for example, will sometimes do hermeneutics when he prepares his Sunday homily. If he were to preach on the parable of the Sower (Mk 4:1-9), for example, he'd want to know the best way to preach that meaning for his Sunday morning congregation.

EXERCISES

A. *Identifying some literary forms.* There are a number of literary forms which have been found in the New Testament writings. Here are some which can be found in the gospels. Listed is the name of the form, a very short description and a reference which will give you an example of it.

Literary form	**Description**	**Example**
parable	a short story drawn from ordinary, everyday life with a religious message	Prodigal Son (Lk 15:11-32)
nature miracle	a sign/miracle which demonstrates Jesus' power over the forces of nature	calming of the storm (Lk 8:22-25)
pronounce-ment story	a passage centering around a very important saying of Jesus	sabbath healing (Mk 3:1-5)
healing story	a sign/miracle where Jesus demonstrates his power over sin by curing a person	cure of the deaf-mute (Mt 9:32-34)
controversy story	a passage in which everything centers around Jesus and his opponents	tribute to Caesar (Mt 22:15-22)

Literary form	Description	Example
riddle	a question or statement which requires thought to understand	Jesus' description of John the Baptist (Mt 11:11)
prayer	a specially worded form used in early church liturgies illustrating a point being made about Jesus	Mary's canticle (Lk 1:46-55)

Exercise: Read the following three passages from Mark's gospel. Summarize them. Then identify which kind of form each one illustrates.

	Summary	*Form*
Mk 1:40-45	______________________ ______________________ ______________________	__________
Mk 4:26-29	______________________ ______________________ ______________________	__________
Mk 12:18-27	______________________ ______________________ ______________________	__________

B. *Hermeneutics.* Please read John 15:1-17. Study the text carefully. Then outline a short talk based on this reading. The talk should be geared to a group of your classmates.

____

SOME HELPFUL BACKGROUND INFORMATION

Language and Texts of the New Testament

Have you ever wondered where the Bible comes from? The first thing to note is that the New Testament was originally written in *koine* or common Greek. Koine Greek was the spoken Greek used as a common language of the Roman Empire in our Lord's day and in the centuries immediately following his death and resurrection. It was the language of the tradesmen, of the soldiers quartered in their barracks. It has a freshness, warmth, shortness and earthiness which is lacking in the classical Greek which Homer, for example, used when he wrote his classics, *The Iliad* and *The Odyssey.*

At first the scribes wrote the New Testament on papyrus, a kind of paper which was made from a reed found in the delta of the Nile River and in parts of Italy. Other writing was done on parchment, which was made from the skins of animals. Papyri and parchments which contain ancient copies of the New Testament are housed in various libraries around the world. Two of the most famous papyri are the John Rylands Greek Papyrus and the Papyrus Bodmer.

Translations

The Bible you use is a translation into English of these papyri, parchments and other ancient copies of the New Testament. For centuries Protestants have been using the very popular King James Version (1611). This is still the most widely used translation around today. Until recently Catholics relied on the Douay Version (1609-1610). Today we have many other good English versions of the Bible translated from the original languages. Here is a list of some of the most popular ones.

1. ***The Revised Standard Version*** (1952). This Protestant translation is now available in an edition which is acceptable to Catholics. It tries to keep the traditional flavor of the older English language translations of the Bible.

2. ***The New English Bible*** (1961). This is an important Protestant translation which attempts to produce "a faithful rendering of the best available Greek text into the current speech of the times."

3. ***Good News for Modern Man*** (NT—1966). This is a Protestant translation in the language of today produced by the American Bible Society.

4. ***The Jerusalem Bible*** (1966). The Jerusalem Bible is the translation of the Bible used in this text. It is an excellent Catholic version which has been translated from the French which in turn has been translated from the original languages. It attempts to render the Bible into the language we use today and provides excellent notes that help the reader understand the text better.

5. ***New American Bible*** (1970). This is another outstanding Catholic translation which attempts to be very close to the meaning of the original text. It tries to be "suitable for liturgical use, private reading, and study."

6. ***New International Bible*** (NT—1973). Another outstanding Protestant version which corresponds to the intent and philosophy of the New American Bible.

To show the different flavor of the various translations, here is a short passage from three of the versions. Compare and contrast the language used to convey the same basic idea from the biblical text. The text given is Luke 8:16-18.

Good News Bible

No one lights a lamp and covers it with a bowl or puts it under a bed. Instead, he puts it on the lampstand, so that people will see the light as they come in. Whatever is hidden away will be brought out into the open, and whatever is covered up will be found and brought to light.

Jerusalem Bible

No one lights a lamp to cover it with a bowl or to put it under a bed. No, he puts it on a lamp-stand so that people may see the light when they come in. For nothing is hidden but it will be made clear, nothing secret but it will be known and brought to light.

New American Bible

No one lights a lamp and puts it under a bushel basket or under a bed; he puts it on a lampstand so that whoever comes in can see it. There is nothing hidden that will not be exposed, nothing concealed that will not be known and brought to light.

SHORT EXERCISE

Read any chapter from three different translations of the New Testament. Note what you like or dislike as you read. Decide which is your favorite version and report to the class why you decided as you did.

Tools for Your Study of the New Testament

1. *Concordance.* Have you ever had the frustrating experience of not being able to find a particular passage in the Bible? A concordance can help you do just that. It lists alphabetically every important word used in the Bible and then gives all the places where the word can be found. For example, suppose you want to find where Jesus said, "You are salt." You would look under the word *salt* in a concordance and there you would find listed all the places it is mentioned in the Bible. Here are some good concordances:

Cruden's Complete Concordance, Zondervan, 1968.

Hartdegen, S., ed., *Nelson's Complete Concordance of the New American Bible,* Nelson, 1977.

2. *Bible atlas.* A bible atlas is full of good maps that will help you get around the New Testament world. Here are two good ones:

Aharoni, Yohanan and Michael Avi-Yonah, *The Macmillan Bible Atlas,* Macmillan, 1968.

Grollenberg, L., *Atlas of the Bible,* Nelson, 1956.

3. *Dictionary.* A dictionary of the Bible will give a good short treatment of many themes, names, places, etc., found in the Bible. One of the best is Father John L. McKenzie's *Dictionary of the Bible* (Macmillan, 1965). Another good, scholarly one is Father Leon-Dufour's *Dictionary of Biblical Theology* (Seabury, 1973).

4. *Synopsis.* A gospel synopsis helps show the New Testament student how the writers of various gospels treat the same event. A synopsis aids in doing this by presenting the three synoptic gospels—Matthew, Mark and Luke—in parallel columns. The most famous one is based on the Revised Standard Version—Burton H. Throckmorton, Jr., *Gospel Parallels* (Nelson, 1961).

5. *New Testament commentary.* A commentary gives you a verse-by-verse explanation of the passage you are reading. There are many excellent ones. Here are three outstanding ones written by Catholic scholars.

Brown, S.S., Raymond, Joseph Fitzmyer, S.J., and Roland Murphy, O. Carm., eds., *Jerome Biblical Commentary,* Prentice-Hall, 1968. An outstanding one-volume work which is a library in itself. It comments on each of the books of the Bible and has some excellent background material as well.

Doubleday New Testament Commentary Series, New York: Doubleday & Co. Inc., 1977. A multi-volume series written especially for the layperson and based on *The Jerusalem Bible.*

New Testament Message, Wilmington, Delaware: Michael Glazier Inc., 1979. A 22-volume commentary by noted Catholic scholars.

USING THE TOOLS

A. With the help of a concordance, find the following passages in the New Testament:

"The proof that you are sons is that God has sent the Spirit of his Son into our hearts: the Spirit that cries, 'Abba, Father.' "

____

"I am the Good Shepherd." ________________________

"I am the Alpha and Omega."________________________

B. With the help of a bible atlas, trace the outline of the city of Jerusalem in Jesus' day. Note at least seven points of major interest.

C. Using any dictionary of the Bible, respond to four of the following:

1. Define the term *disciple.*
2. List the 12 apostles.
3. Where is the city of Magdala?
4. Define the term *parable.*
5. Who was Gamaliel?
6. What does *kingdom of God* mean?
7. What is the salt content of the Dead Sea?
8. Identify the term *Gehenna.*

D. Read Mark 10:17-22, Jesus' encounter with the rich young man. Then read any New Testament commentary that deals with this passage and report to the class any new insights you gained.

E. Choose three scripture readings that you would use for the funeral Mass of a friend or a grandparent. Discuss why you chose these particular passages. How did you locate them?

SUMMARY

To aid your review, each of the chapters in this book will contain a few statements summarizing the main points of the chapter. The main ideas to remember from Chapter 1 are the following:

1. The New Testament traces its origin to the good news of Jesus Christ. This good news was summarized in the kerygma, the core preaching about Jesus who is the Messiah, the Son of God in whom we have eternal life.

2. The New Testament was written over a period of roughly 60 years. It contains 27 different books. The two chief forms of writing found there are the gospels and epistles.

3. The New Testament grew through three stages: the period of Jesus' historical life, the period of the oral transmission of the good news, and the period of the writings themselves.

4. The canon of the New Testament refers to the official list of books considered inspired by the church.

5. Methods of studying the New Testament include historical, source, form and redaction criticism, and also hermeneutics.

6. The New Testament was originally written in koine Greek and has been translated into English many times. *The Jerusalem Bible* and the *New American Bible* are two important Catholic translations.

7. Major tools for studying the Bible include concordances, atlases, biblical dictionaries, synopses and commentaries.

EVALUATION

At the end of each chapter there will be a short quiz or test to check your grasp of some of the material in the chapter. Good luck on this first one.

1. Define the following terms:

   didache: ______________________________

   inspiration: ______________________________

2. Suppose you are reading a passage from John's gospel and don't understand what the passage means. Where would be the *best* place to look for help?
   ____ concordance ____ commentary ____ atlas ____ dictionary of the Bible ____ synopsis

3. Briefly outline the key preaching made about Jesus in the period of oral transmission.

   ____

   ____

   ____

4. Which of the following statements refers to historical criticism? to hermeneutics? to redaction criticism?
   a. Searching for the meaning of the New Testament text for today's Christians.

   ____

   b. Discovering the Jesus behind the texts. ______________
   c. Considering how different authors used the same kind of material.

   ____

5. What is the relationship between the gospel of Luke and Acts of the Apostles?

   ____

6. Which three gospels can be read together; that is, which are the synoptic gospels?

   ____

7. Which of the following letters was *not* written by Paul?
   1 Corinthians Hebrews Philippians Romans
8. List and discuss a few points on how we should pray based on New Testament teaching.

   ____

   ____

   ____

9. The good news of Jesus demands ____________ on our part.
10. Put the following New Testament writings in chronological order from the earliest written (1) to the latest (5).
    ____ John ____ Luke ____ 1 Peter ____ 1 Thessalonians
    ____ Mark

READING GOD'S WORD

Please read Paul's letter to Philemon. Then answer these questions.

Who wrote this epistle?____________________________

To whom is this letter addressed? ________________________

What does the author pray for? ________________________

On whose behalf is the author writing? __________________

What kind of relationship does the author have with this person?

____

Where is the author? ______________________________

What station in life does the person for whom the author writes occupy?

____

What does the author ask for on the behalf of this person?

____

How does the letter end? ______________________________

Discuss these questions:

1. Does the author pronounce against slavery? Why or why not?
2. Does the author take the "sting" out of slavery? Explain.

Research:

Consult a biblical dictionary and report on slavery in biblical times.

PRAYER REFLECTION

The author of Philemon prays that the peace and grace of the Father and our Lord Jesus Christ be with his fellow Christians. Let us pause and think of some friends, our parents, our teachers, our brothers and sisters, and pray that Jesus' peace and grace be with them.

Oh Lord, bless our loved ones.
Shower them with your gifts,
your close friendship, your joy, your peace.
Help us see you as our Abba, our Father, who loves us.
Help us realize that we are loved by you.
Thank you, Lord, for your warmth, your kindness, your love.
Thank you for telling us that we are worth something.
Praise be to you. Amen.

2

Background for Reading the New Testament: Understanding the New Testament World

Now at this time Caesar Augustus issued a decree for a census of the whole world to be taken. This census—the first—took place while Quirinius was governor of Syria, and everyone went to his own town to be registered. So Joseph set out from the town of Nazareth in Galilee and traveled up to Judaea, to the town of David called Bethlehem, since he was of David's House and line, in order to be registered together with Mary, his betrothed, who was with child.

—Luke 2:1-6

This chapter opens with an important quote from Luke's gospel. In it, Luke tries to situate Jesus' birth at a particular time in a particular place. He mentions two people who played key roles in the birth of the Messiah: Joseph and Mary. These details are important because they underscore the fact that Jesus was a real, historical person.

Luke pinpoints Jesus in time and place. Jesus and his story are not based on some legend lost in the mist of prehistory. No, Jesus lived in Palestine in the first century of our era. Caesar Augustus ruled the Roman Empire when Jesus was born; Tiberius was emperor when he died. Jesus walked dusty roads in a country far distant from Rome. He taught in synagogues where first-century Jews gathered to pray to their God. He himself was a Jew who knew the scriptures of his people, who shared many of their beliefs, who lived their customs.

The New Testament writings make much more sense to us if we are somewhat familiar with the world in which they were written. This world was the world of Jesus and his people and the world of the

Roman Empire. The purpose of this chapter is to take a brief look at the background in which the New Testament took root and flourished. We will do that by discussing the following topics:

- the history of God's covenant with the Jews (the Old Testament background)
- the geography of the New Testament world
- Judaism in Jesus' time

Time spent mastering this background chapter is time well spent. The more we know about Jesus' world the more we will appreciate his word and the words about him recorded in the New Testament.

TWO OLD TESTAMENT STARTERS

A. *Getting into the Old Testament story.* One of the best ways to review the background to the New Testament is to see how God worked in the lives of some of the great heroes of the Old Testament period. Here is a list of some of those heroes. With one or two classmates, please do the following:

a. Select one of the names listed.
b. Consult a bible dictionary, an atlas, a biblical encyclopedia and other resource books to get the following basic information about your hero:
   (1) Does the person's name have any special meaning?
   (2) When did the person live?
   (3) List several important beliefs, actions and persons in your hero's life.
c. As a class, arrange in chronological order the heroes selected for discussion. With your partner(s), give a short summary of what you learned.

Some Bible Heroes and Heroines

Abraham	Hosea	Samuel	Nehemiah	Rebecca
Isaac	Aaron	David	Ezekiel	Deborah
Jacob	Moses	Jonathan	Gideon	Ruth
Solomon	Jeremiah	Samson	Simeon	Esther
Amos	Joshua	Micah	Sarah	Miriam
Elizabeth	Judith			

B. *What do you believe?* Listed here are some of the major beliefs that many Jews of Jesus' time held to be true. What do you think of them? Do they make sense to you? Check the box which most accurately reflects your belief.

	I strongly believe this	I believe this	I don't believe this	I don't know about this
1. Everything that God made is good.				
2. There is only one God and he loves me.				
3. Devils exist.				
4. Angels exist.				
5. God will punish evil-doers.				
6. The good person will be rewarded in the afterlife.				
7. God is involved in the history of the world.				
8. God is deeply involved in my history.				
9. God is good.				
10. God forgives sin.				

Discussion:

a. What does each of the statements mean to you? Why did you choose as you did?

b. Share your choices with your classmates.

c. If you checked either column one or two for No. 8, write a short essay on how this is true. You may wish to share this with one other person.

THE OLD TESTAMENT STORY

The Old Testament story is, above all else, the story of God's love affair with his children. Clearly and forcefully Genesis, the first book listed in the Bible, reveals a loving God who formed humans from the mud of the earth and breathed life into them. The Bible reveals a God who from the very beginning shared his life and his love.

TIME LINE		*SUGGESTED READINGS*	*THE STORY*
B.C.			
1900	Abraham & the Patriarchs	*Abraham* Gn 12; 15; 16-19; 21-22	1. *I call you by name.* Mysteriously and wondrously God called a wandering nomad, Abraham, to true worship of the one God. God blessed Abraham and promised to him a people—a people who would represent God before others. This call and response is called *covenant,* a kind of contract between God and his people characterized by loving kindness. For his part, Abraham and his descendents—great heroes like Isaac, Jacob and Joseph—were to obey and worship the one true God before the nations.
1700	Hebrews in Egypt	*Joseph* Gn 37; 39-45	2. *From slavery to freedom.* Salvation history records that famine drove the Hebrews into Egypt where over the course of years they were enslaved. God, however, remained faithful to his people and chose Moses to lead them to freedom. In the desert sojourn, God renewed his convenant on Mt. Sinai. There he promised to his chosen ones a land flowing with milk and honey. In return, the Hebrews were to live the Law (summarized in the Ten Commandments) as
1500	Slavery & oppression	*Moses* Ex 1-6:13; 7-11; 12:21-41; 13:17-22; 14; 15:19-27; 19-20; 24; 32-34:9	

1300	Exodus	
		Jos 3-4
1200	Into the Promised Land	
1100	Judges rule in Yahweh's name	Jgs 13-16
1000	A united kingdom	*David* 1 Sm 16-19 2 Sm 11-13
900	A divided kingdom	

a concrete way of showing their love for God. The history of the desert wandering is the story of many failures of the Hebrews to love God. In their movement toward a perfect love of God they would often fall short of their goal. But God never failed them. He was continuously faithful to them. This desert experience foreshadowed the rest of the Old Testament story.

3. *Into the land and a kingdom.* With God's help Joshua crossed the Jordan River and conquered the Promised Land while forming an alliance with 12 tribes. The people assumed the name *Israelites* with Yahweh as their own true God. As the land became one both politically and religiously under a group of men known as the Judges, the people clamored for a king of their own. God granted their wish. The greatest of these kings was David (c. 1000-961 B.C.). He united the kingdom with Jerusalem as the capital; brought peace, culture and prosperity; and enriched the spiritual life of the people. David was the ideal king who brought the everlasting hope that one day Yahweh would send a Messiah-king who would rule with true justice and establish God's peace everywhere.
4. *The kingdom falls apart.* David's son Solomon built the Temple in Jerusalem. It became the center of worship. Under his sons,

TIME LINE		*SUGGESTED READINGS*
800		
722	Northern kingdom falls to Assyria	
		Hos 2:4-3:5 Am 2:6-16 Jer 52:4-16
587	Jerusalem destroyed	
		Is 52:13-53:12
537	Babylonian Captivity	
400	Ezra the scribe	

THE STORY

however, the people turned to idolatry, the worship of false gods. The united kingdom came apart. The northern kingdom fell to Assyria in 722 B.C.; the southern kingdom of Judah was overrun by Babylonia in 587 B.C. Great prophets warned against infidelity to the covenant (Jeremiah) and oppression of the poor (Amos). They called their people to faithfulness, but their word went unheeded. Never again would Israel be politically one, although the hope for a Messiah never died.

5. *Captivity again and return*. Many of the Jews in the southern kingdom were carried off to Babylon as slaves. Only God speaking through prophets such as the author of the second part of the book of Isaiah kept alive the flame of hope of an eventual return to the Promised Land. Trust in Yahweh's word was vindicated when the Jews once again returned to Israel to reestablish their worship of God in Jerusalem. Attention was focused on their religion; for example, scripture was written down for the first time. But political independence was lost: The Jews were now ruled by Persia. The Temple was rededicated (516 B.C.) and men such as Nehemiah and Ezra reminded the people of their cove-

333 — Alexander the Great

Greek rule

1 Mc 6-7

165 — Maccabean Revolt

63 — Rome conquers

nant with God. Fidelity to the Law helped to unite the people.

6. *More oppression and revolt.* Persian rule lasted until Alexander the Great (333 B.C.) came on the scene. His attempts to *hellenize,* that is, to bring Greek culture to his empire, were resisted with mixed success in the Holy Land. Jews kept their religion alive through Temple worship and by meeting in prayer houses called synagogues. In 165 B.C., a great desecration of the Temple took place under the arrogant Antiochus Epiphanes who attempted to wipe out Judaism. His outrageous act led to the revolt of the Maccabean family who helped save the Jewish religion from the influence of the pagans. For a time Israel had a kind of political independence. But internal squabbles among the leaders and priests led to the formation of various religious sects like the Pharisees and the Essenes who tried to live strictly according to the Mosaic Law.
7. *The Romans.* In the midst of persecution and rule by foreigners, the hope for a Messiah never died. The Maccabees revived the hope that one day God would establish his justice and rule the whole earth (Zec 14:9). The Romans under Pompey, however, abolished Jewish rule forever when they conquered Palestine in 63 B.C. They allowed Herod, a half-Jew, to

	Herod the Great rules Israel	Mt 2
4-6 A.D.	Jesus is born	
30	Jesus dies	
	Paul preaches	
66	Revolt against Rome	
70	Temple destroyed	

rule at their whim. Herod was a great builder who undertook the reconstruction of the Temple. He died in 4 B.C. dividing his kingdom among his three sons. One son, Herod Antipas, ruled in Jesus' home district of Galilee. Another son was exiled because of his cruel rule. He was replaced by a Roman prefect in A.D. 6. One such prefect, Pontius Pilate, ruled in Judaea and Samaria from A.D. 26 to 36. The Jews believed that the Romans were against God. Eventually their hatred of the Romans led to an unsuccessful revolt (A.D. 66-70) which ended in the destruction of the Temple. The Pharisees survived this revolt and became the leaders of the Judaism which was to survive.

In this period Caesar Augustus brought the great *Pax Romana*—the Peace of Rome. And, of course, during this era, God sent the Prince of Peace—Jesus Christ—to fulfill his covenant of love.

THE STORY CONTINUED

A. *Old Testament readings.* Divide the passages listed above among your classmates. Read them and summarize the story in a class presentation.

B. *The good news of the New Testament.* The time line you have just studied summarizes the story of God's love affair with his people. The New Testament brings this story to its happy ending in Jesus Christ. Here are the highlights of that story which you will study firsthand when you read the New Testament. The good news is expressed in a way to involve you because it is meant for you. Put an "X" somewhere on the line below each statement to indicate your present attitude to the good news. An "X" at the left end of the line indicates that you don't really know what this statement means; an "X" at the right end of the line means that the statement means a lot to you and affects your life. You may be somewhere in-between.

1. God loves me and everyone with a tremendous love.
   I don't know ________________________ Means a lot
2. God doesn't make junk. All that he makes (including me) is very good.
   I don't know ________________________ Means a lot
3. God calls me into eternal union with him.
   I don't know ________________________ Means a lot
4. God wants me to accept his love and change the direction of my life.
   I don't know ________________________ Means a lot
5. Jesus is God the Father's presence for me. He is God's love incarnate.
   I don't know ________________________ Means a lot
6. The Holy Spirit opens me up to God's love and truth. He gives me the strength and help on my journey to the Father.
   I don't know ________________________ Means a lot
7. Jesus tells me that life is a paradox: Life comes through death; we receive when we give.
   I don't know ________________________ Means a lot
8. The good news tells us that good will eventually triumph over evil, that love will conquer hate, that life will conquer death.
   I don't know ________________________ Means a lot
9. As a result of all this good news, the Christian is a person of hope. I hope.
   I don't know ________________________ Means a lot

Sharing: Share your responses to some of these items. Discuss what you think each statement means. If you can, give examples from your life.

THE NEW TESTAMENT WORLD

The Holy Land

In our Lord's day, what today is called the country of Israel was most often referred to as the Promised Land, the Holy Land, the Land of Israel, the Land of Judah or simply, the Land. The Greeks called it Palestine after the Philistines, the seafaring pirates who inhabited the northern coastal areas. (This designation was insulting to the Jews.) Roughly the shape of a rectangle, this land stretches barely 145 miles north to south and from 25 miles wide in the north to its greatest width of 87 miles near the Dead Sea in the south.

The Holy Land has always occupied a strategic place in world history. It was considered the keystone of the "fertile crescent." As such, it was a crossroads for Egyptian expansion east and north, and for Syrian and Persian moves westward. Later it became an attractive target for the political conquests of Greece and Rome.

The land is a geographer's delight. Within a few hours' time the well-seasoned traveler can go from 9,000-foot-high mountain ranges that rise in the far north to a barren desert in the east and arable lands on the western coastal strip. The Jordan River rises in the northern mountains, widens into the marvelous Sea of Galilee, narrows through a fertile valley and winds up in the saltiest of all bodies of water—the Dead Sea. This body of water is the lowest point below sea level on the face of the earth. It has a salt content of 25%, six times that of the saltiest ocean; it is impossible to sink in it.

Galilee in the north was a relatively rich land of fertile, rolling hills. There farmers and shepherds could be seen living off the land. The freshwater lake found there provided a livelihood for many fishermen like Peter. In contrast, Judaea in the south was a dry, barren, craggy land. In its center, lofted on two hills 2400 to 2255 feet above sea level, was Jerusalem, the political, economic and religious center of Judaism. In Jerusalem Jews earned a living at a number of trades: merchants in wool, leather workers, olive oil processors, bakers and butchers, manufacturers of ointments and resins, building tradesmen, traders of grain and other foodstuffs and various trades associated with the Temple and the Jewish religion (scribes, for example, who interpreted the Law).

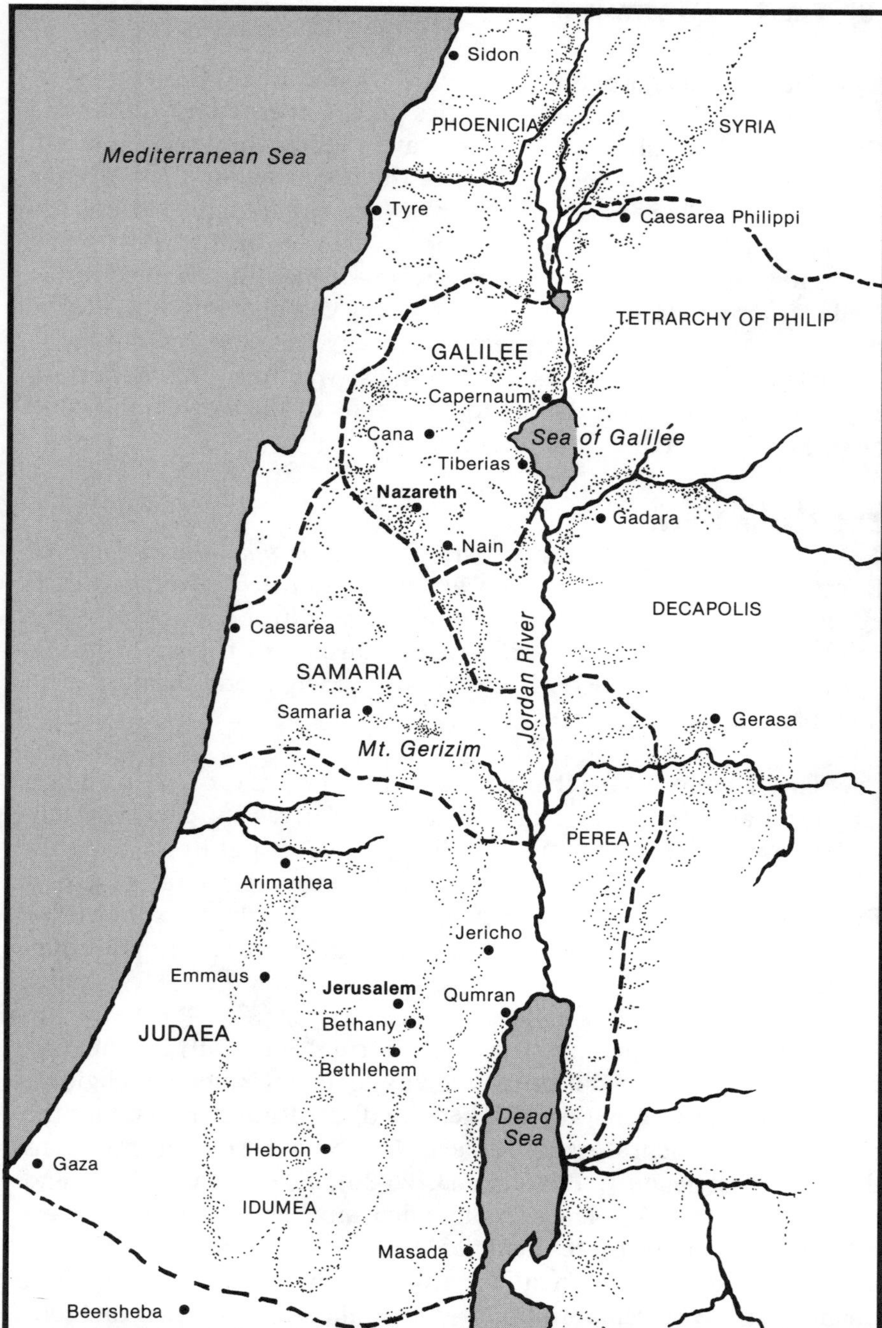

Map 1: The Holy Land in Jesus' Day

The synoptic gospels (Matthew, Mark and Luke) locate most of Jesus' public life in Galilee. Cities like Capernaum, Cana and Nazareth had an important role to play in Jesus' ministry. Nazareth was the hometown of Jesus. Many of the important and picturesque details which color Jesus' parables had their origin in his keen observations of life in Galilee: birds of the air, flowers brilliantly arraying the fields, barns filled with grain, the sower planting his seed in the fields, fishing nets straining under a heavy catch. The gospels agree that Jesus was born in Bethlehem in Judaea and made the journey to Jerusalem where he met his death. And it was from this important city that his disciples preached to the "ends of the world" the good news of salvation and Jesus' resurrection.

The Roman Empire

At the time of Jesus, the *Pax Romana*—the Peace of Rome—prevailed. The Empire was known as the civilized world. It extended as far as Great Britain in northern Europe to Egypt in the southeastern part of the Mediterranean basin. All tribes not in this territory were considered *barbarians,* uncivilized peoples who mumbled strange languages.

The Empire was characterized by the rise of a common language, an intricate system of roads, a relatively sure legal system and an ever-present and strong military force. It put down banditry and piracy so that trade and communication took place rather easily. Peace was welcome in the ancient world and helped explain how Christianity flourished so rapidly around the Mediterranean Sea during the first century.

Rome was sometimes harsh in its rule, especially in quieting rebellious peoples. It did tolerate many different kinds of religions, though. The Jews generally disliked the direct Roman rule under the prefects and procurators in Judaea. The New Testament mentions three of these leaders: Pilate (A.D. 26-36), Felix (A.D. 52-60) and Festus (A.D. 60-62). They commanded auxiliary forces in Judaea made up of non-Jewish residents of Palestine and Syria. For the most part these troops were greatly resented by the Jews. Rome allowed the highest Jewish religious body—the Sanhedrin—considerable self-rule in religious and minor political matters. However, the right of

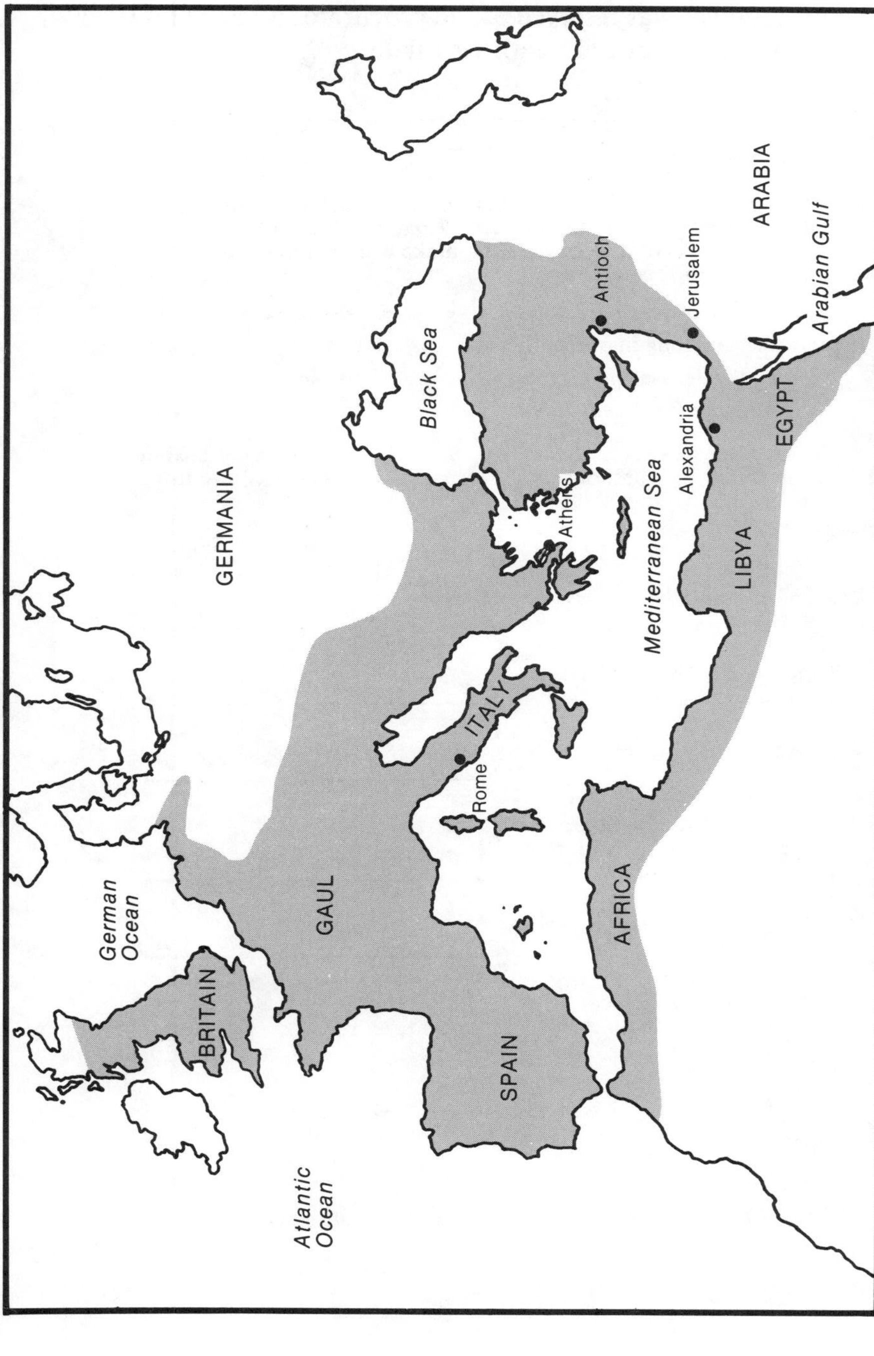

Map 2: The Roman Empire in Christ's Time

capital punishment was reserved to the procurator alone. This is why Jesus was ultimately put to death by Pilate.

SOME EXERCISES

1. Using a dictionary of the Bible or a book like Father Henri Daniel-Rops' *Daily Life in the Time of Jesus* (Ann Arbor, Michigan: Servant Books, 1981), make a short report on one of the following topics:

   a. social classes in Israel
   b. schooling in our Lord's day
   c. the Jerusalem Temple
   d. New Testament foods
   e. occupations
   f. Samaria
   g. Sanhedrin

2. *Jesus and some New Testament cities.* Use your bibles to answer the following questions. The references you will need are listed below the questions.

Questions	*City*	*Bible Passage*
1. Where did Jesus perform his first sign?	________	________
2. What city was his hometown?	________	________
3. Where did his friend Lazarus live?	________	________
4. To what city was he traveling when Peter confessed him as the Messiah?	________	________
5. What city became his headquarters?	________	________
6. Where did he appear to a couple of his disciples?	________	________

The References

Jn 11:1-44	Lk 24:13-35	Mk 8:27-33
Mt 2:19-23	Mt 4:12-22	Jn 2:1-11

Map

Using the map on page 57, locate each of the cities above.

JUDAISM IN JESUS' TIME

The New Testament was born out of a Jewish world. Jesus was a Jew and so were most of his early followers. Christians of the first century by and large saw their religious movement as a fulfillment of Judaism. To begin to understand the New Testament it is necessary to take a look at the Jewish religion of our Lord's day. Here we will examine the different religious groups and some of the major beliefs of the Jews. This background will help us read the New Testament with more appreciation.

Religious Groups

An interesting character of the New Testament era was the colorful Jewish historian Josephus. He wrote his history of the Jewish people to show the Romans that the Jews were good people with an advanced civilization. In that history he mentioned four sects or "philosophies": the Sadducees, the Pharisees, the Essenes and the Zealots.

1. ***Sadducees.*** This group got its name from Sadok, the priest whom Solomon appointed to take charge of the ark of the covenant (1 Kgs 2:35). The Sadducees were the priestly aristocracy who cared for Temple practices and worship. Their center of operation was Jerusalem. They were generally wealthy and part of the establishment and so did not want to "rock the boat" for fear of losing their positions of prestige and power. They were intent on not upsetting the Romans.

Conservative in their theological beliefs, the Sadducees accepted as inspired only the Torah, the first five books of the Old Testament. Anything not found there was not considered authoritative. For example, they did not believe in the relatively new teaching of the resurrection of the body.

The Sadducees—in the persons of the priests and elders—were the key figures who argued against Jesus at his trial.

2. ***Pharisees.*** This group was probably the most influential

group of Jesus' day. They got their name from a word which means "separated ones." The Pharisees were a group of laymen; many seem to have been middle-class artisans, officials, traders and other service people. They separated themselves from other Jews in that they tried to live the ancient Law fully and apart from Gentile influence.

Great stress was put on exact religious observances, especially in regard to purity and *tithing* (that is, giving one-tenth of their income, produce, and the like, to the priests and Levites). The Pharisees tended to look down on Jews who did not observe the Law as carefully as they did.

In following the Law, the Pharisees developed an elaborate system of interpretation which they held to be almost as sacred as the Law itself. These interpretations sometimes missed the spirit of the Law and even resulted in real harm being done to persons. Jesus came in conflict with some Pharisees both because of their attitude of looking down on others and for some of their interpretations of the Law.

In theological beliefs the Pharisees were more modern than the Sadducees. They believed in the resurrection and judgment of the dead. They held this belief in common with Jesus who, on occasion, would dine with them (Lk 11:37, 14:1). After the Romans destroyed the Temple in A.D. 70, this group saved Judaism by regrouping. They met in a rabbinical council at Jamnia on the Mediterranean Sea in the year 90 and collected together the Hebrew scriptures. The Judaism that exists today is the descendent of the Pharisees of the first century.

3. *Essenes.* This group was responsible for writing the Dead Sea scrolls. They are not mentioned in the New Testament, though Josephus and Pliny, the Roman historian, do write about them. This group has gained a lot of attention in recent years because of the discovery of the scrolls. They were founded by someone known as the Teacher of Righteousness. They believed that the Jerusalem priesthood and Temple worship were impure and that the Law was not being lived properly by most Jews.

Many of them withdrew to a desert community where they lived a rigorous life. Most did not get married. They shared goods in common and lived a life of ritual purity, cleansing themselves often throughout the day. New members went through an elaborate initiation cermony.

The Essenes were an *apocalyptic* group. The term *apocalyptic* refers to the belief that all history can be divided into two great ages: an Old Age of death and injustice, and a New Age of God's kingdom with its peace and mercy. Groups like the Essenes thought that the New Age would be ushered in by some dramatic, catastrophic act—a major battle between the forces of light and the forces of darkness. They combed the Jewish scriptures for signs of when this event would take place, and they lived lives of extreme purity so that when the day came they would be found on God's side.

4. ***Zealots.*** At least one of Jesus' apostles—Simon—was a Zealot. Zealots were also known as *Sicarii* (which means dagger carriers). They hated the foreign rule of the Romans with extreme passion. They believed in violent action against their enemies because they believed that they were engaged in a holy war which was about to usher in the New Age. This apocalyptic group wanted to help Yahweh firsthand in the destruction of Jewish enemies.

Scholars believe that the Zealots got their start when Quirinius, the governor of Syria, called for a census in the Holy Land (Lk 2:2). This fanatic nationalist sect had a following in Galilee in Jesus' day, but its greatest success was in fomenting the disastrous revolt against Rome in 66-70. Some Zealots survived and kept the revolt alive at Masada (until 73). Interestingly enough, there was a second revolt against Rome in 132-135 under a strong leader whom many Jews thought was the Messiah. The leader was a man named Simon *bar-Kokhba,* which means the "son of a star." The revolt ended in total disaster for the Jews; from that time on they were forbidden to set foot in the holy city of Jerusalem.

READING DEEPER

A. *Jesus as a debater.* In his ministry, Jesus often conflicted with the Pharisees and Sadducees. They often tested Jesus and criticized him. Here are two very important places in the New Testament where Jesus engaged in debate with these groups. Please read the passages and then answer the questions. Share responses.

Pharisees: Read Mark 7:1-23

1. What didn't the disciples do? (vv. 1-2) ____________________

2. Why was this a problem for the Pharisees? (vv. 3-6) ____________________

3. What commandment does Jesus say they go around? (vv. 9-10)

4. How do the Pharisees make an excuse to avoid the obligation of this commandment? (vv. 11-18)

5. From where does evil come? (vv. 14-20) ____________________

6. List several actions that come from evil intentions. (v. 22) ______

Sadducees: Read Mark 12:18-27

1. What case did the Sadducees put before Jesus? (vv. 19-23) ______

2. Who established the law quoted by the Sadducees? (v. 19) ______

3. Was their question to Jesus sincere? Why or why not? (v. 18)

Jesus gives the Sadducees a two-part answer. First, he answers their question on its own merits.

4. How does he respond? (vv. 25-26) ____________________

Second, Jesus shows that he believes in the resurrection by quoting the same person as the Sadducees.

5. What is Jesus' argument in support of the resurrection? (vv. 26-27)

____

Note: The Book of Moses = Torah = Pentateuch

Discuss: How does Jesus beat the Sadducees at their own game?

B. *Your own version of the Present Age vs. the New Age of God's kingdom.* List the five most important characteristics of our age. For example, you might say that the present age is characterized by great scientific achievements or marked by great prejudice. Then list five traits that you think will come upon the scene when God's kingdom is fully established. For example, you might say the future age will be marked by equality between the sexes.

Present Age	*Age of God's Kingdom*
1. ____________________	1. ____________________
____________________	____________________
2. ____________________	2. ____________________
____________________	____________________
3. ____________________	3. ____________________
____________________	____________________
4. ____________________	4. ____________________
____________________	____________________
5. ____________________	5. ____________________

Discuss:

a. Compile a class list of characteristics. Discuss and agree on about 10 of the best traits for each era.

b. Do any of the traits of the New Age correspond to what you hope to happen in your own personal future?

c. Can you or your classmates do anything *right now* to help God's kingdom grow, to help the traits of the New Age come alive? Discuss and explain.

____

Some Beliefs

You can tell a lot about a people by examining their beliefs. Here are some of the more significant beliefs held by Jews in New Testament times.

The Torah. For all the various Jewish groups discussed above, the Law (Torah) was very important. Written down in the Pentateuch (the Old Testament books of Genesis, Exodus, Leviticus, Numbers and Deuteronomy), the Torah was much more than a dead letter. It was the heart of the Jewish religion. Jews believed that by living it they were responding to God's incredible covenant of love. It influenced Jewish history, culture, morality and worship. Jesus himself respected the Law and called on his followers to live it fully

(Mt. 5:17-20). Even today it greatly influences Jewish life.

The Messiah. Above all else, first-century Judaism was a messianic age. People hoped for a king, an anointed one of God, who would usher in God's promised kingdom. Expectations on how the Messiah would come, though, differed widely. Zealots believed that a revolutionary military leader would impose God's kingdom by violently overthrowing Israel's enemies. The literature of the Essenes pointed to two different kinds of Messiah: a kingly Messiah who would engage in battle against the forces of darkness, and a priestly Messiah who would purge false worship in Jerusalem.

The Pharisees thought that if they kept to the letter of the Law, Yahweh would look favorably on the people and send the Messiah-king. Little did any of these groups expect that the Messiah would be a humble carpenter who would emerge from a distant village far from Jerusalem—Jesus of Nazareth who associated with sinners and who taught his countrymen to love their enemies.

The kingdom of God. Although the term *kingdom* or *reign* of God was not as used in Old Testament times as it was in the New Testament, the idea behind it was central to Jewish belief. The kingdom of God is "the acceptance of God's will by everyone." When people know God as he has revealed himself through the Jews and later most perfectly through Jesus Christ, then magnificent things will happen. Justice will reign. Material needs will be taken care of. God's peace will extend throughout the world.

We Christians believe that Jesus Christ has mysteriously inaugurated the reign of God. We also believe that we have a duty to help extend God's kingdom by living a Christlike life and preaching the good news. Finally, we look forward in hope to a day when the kingdom will be *fully* established.

Judgment and resurrection. From around the second century B.C. most Jews believed that God would judge the dead and would reward the good and punish the evil. The prophet Daniel argued strongly for the resurrection of good people who "shall live forever" (Dn 12:1-3). Jesus, of course, believed in the resurrection of the dead and Christians today hold the resurrection as a core doctrine. We believe that our resurrection will take place precisely because we are joined to the one who has conquered sin and death: Jesus Christ, Son of God.

Spirit world. From early times, Jews believed in heavenly messengers. Belief in angels grew in the period between the writing of the Old and New Testaments—a period that produced noninspired but important books such as Jubilees, Enoch and the Dead Sea scrolls. This literature divided angels into groups, gave them names and described some of their functions; for example, appearing in human form as Raphael did in the book of Tobias. The New Testament mentions both angels and devils frequently. Jews thought that various demons warred against God by being the sources of sickness, temptation and sin. Jesus cast out many devils and saw his own suffering as a war against the evil one—Satan (Jn 12:31)

Forgiveness of sin. The Jews believed that the Temple sacrifices could forgive sin if a person repented and showed his or her repentance by praying, giving alms to the poor, and fasting. They also believed that a sinner's death, if accepted as God's will, could wipe out his or her sin.

Thus Temple worship was important to the Jews. Jerusalem was the center of *one* sacrifice which took place at *one* place to symbolize belief in *one* God. For most Jews, though, the synagogue was the ordinary center of worship. The synagogue was a meeting place where prayers and the reading and interpretation of the scriptures took place. Jesus often participated in synagogue service and Paul preached in them extensively. Jesus, however, did not limit forgiveness of sin to Temple sacrifices. Christians believe it is Jesus' own suffering, death, resurrection and glorification that forgives sin.

AN EXERCISE IN INTERPRETATION

Earlier in the chapter the point was made that the Pharisees developed an elaborate system of interpretation of the Law. They tried to update it and make it meaningful. Their commentary on the Law can be found in a book called the *Talmud.* The Talmud preserves much rich tradition taught not only by the Pharisees but by other Jewish rabbis from about 200 B.C. to A.D. 450. With your classmates, create your own commentary or interpretation of some of the Old Testament laws, specifically some of the Ten Commandments. Make some statements about what the commandments should mean today to a group of your friends. Some examples are given.

First commandment: I am Yahweh. . . . You shall have no gods except me.

Interpretations:

1. Don't worship your stereo.
2. What people think of you is not the supreme good.
3. ______________________________
4. ______________________________
5. ______________________________
6. ______________________________

Fifth commandment: You shall not kill.

Interpretations:

1. Drive safely.
2. Avoid harmful, addictive drugs.
3. ______________________________
4. ______________________________
5. ______________________________
6. ______________________________

Seventh commandment: You shall not steal.

Interpretations:

1. Shoplifting is not all right.
2. Cheating is out.
3. ______________________________
4. ______________________________
5. ______________________________
6. ______________________________

Eighth commandment: You shall not bear false witness against your neighbor.

Interpretations:

1. Watch your tongue when talking about others.
2. Speak up for a friend.
3. ______________________________
4. ______________________________
5. ______________________________
6. ______________________________

SUMMARY

1. The Old Testament is the story of God's covenant with Israel. It began with Yahweh's promise to Abraham to fashion from him a special people.

2. The covenant between God and Israel was renewed on Mt. Sinai after the deliverance from Egypt (the Exodus). Over the course of years the Jews were given a land and a monarchy with David the ideal king. God's people failed to live the terms of the covenant, however. The kingdom was divided. The north fell to Assyria in 722 B.C., and the southern kingdom fell to Babylonia in 587 B.C.

3. Yahweh sustained his people during the Babylonian captivity and eventually led them back to the Holy Land. Temple worship resumed under men like Ezra and Nehemiah. But the political situation was never the same; first the Persians, then the Greeks and finally the Romans ruled in Israel. Throughout the Old Testament period the hope for a Messiah remained steadfast.

4. The Holy Land was a crucial territory for the major world empires. Its rich and diversified geography supported many trades in New Testament times. From the Holy Land early Christian missionaries spread the good news throughout the Roman Empire, a vast territory united by common language, roads and the famous *Pax Romana*.

5. The major Jewish religious sects in the first century were the Sadducees, Pharisees, Essenes and Zealots.

6. In New Testament times the Torah (Law) was most important for the Jewish religion. Most Jews expected and hoped for a Messiah. They believed in resurrection and final judgment, forgiveness of sin and the existence of angels and devils.

EVALUATION

Directions: Identify the items in column 1 by matching them with the descriptions in column 2. Put the letter from column 2 in the spaces provided.

1. ____ Caesar Augustus
2. ____ Solomon
3. ____ Josephus
4. ____ Talmud
5. ____ synagogue
6. ____ Torah
7. ____ Masada
8. ____ Babylonian captivity
9. ____ Essenes
10. ____ Pharisees
11. ____ Sadducees
12. ____ Zealots
13. ____ Jerusalem Temple
14. ____ covenant
15. ____ Maccabean revolt

a. prayer house
b. the Law
c. God's promise of loving kindness
d. 587-537 B.C.
e. center of Jewish worship
f. sect which cooperated with the Romans
g. *Pax Romana*
h. sect which instigated the Jewish Revolt in A.D. 66-70
i. approximately 165 B.C.
j. Jewish fortress
k. sect which lived at Qumran
l. ancestors of today's Jews
m. builder of the first Temple
n. history of the Jews
o. commentary on the Law

READING GOD'S WORD

From this chapter through Chapter 6, you will be reading about the great Christian missionary St. Paul. His story is recorded in Acts. We begin with Paul's conversion, one of the major events in the early history of the church. Paul, then known as Saul, had been a strict Pharisee who had persecuted Christians. His dramatic conversion and acceptance of Jesus colored the rest of his life. His faith can be traced to this powerful event.

Read about his conversion in Acts 9:1-30.

Then answer these questions on your reading.

What was Saul's plan? ______________________

What happened to Saul on his way to Damascus? ______________________

____

From what city was Saul? ______________________

Why was Ananias afraid to go to Saul? ______________________

____

How did Saul become a Christian? ______________________

____

What was the theme of Saul's early preaching? ______________________

____

How did people react to the transformed Saul? ______________________

____

How did Saul escape the city? ______________________

Who helped Saul in Jerusalem? ______________________

Who plotted against him? ______________________

PRAYER REFLECTION

Throughout his entire ministry Paul put his trust in the Lord, just as the Israelites did throughout the Old Testament period. You have seen how the psalms celebrated this trust in God. For example, Psalm 146 emphasizes our need to trust in God to help us. You may wish to prayerfully read that psalm here. Then write your own prayer reflection in the spirit of the psalm. Here is an example:

Praise God!
O Lord, I won't put my trust in passing things:
what people think of me, the latest possessions,
good grades, money.
These things are passing and have no lasting value.

No, Lord, I look to you to comfort me:
to support me when my friends abandon me,
to be at my side when I'm lonely,
to help me through the rough times of daily temptations,
to let me know that I'm not crazy when
I try to do the right thing.

You, Lord, are the source of my life. You are everything.
Thanks for the life you give me.
Thanks for the talents with which you have blessed me.
Thanks for everything.

Stay with me, Lord, to guide and strengthen me. Amen.

3

Gospel of Mark—
Call to Discipleship

> *Jesus and his disciples left for the villages round Caesarea Philippi. On the way he put this question to his disciples, "Who do people say I am?" And they told him. "John the Baptist," they said, "others Elijah; others again, one of the prophets." "But you," he asked "who do you say I am?" Peter spoke up and said to him, "You are the Christ." And he gave them strict orders not to tell anyone about him.*
>
> —Mark 8:27-30

Our study of the New Testament begins with Mark's gospel, the earliest written of the four gospels. We begin here rather than with any of the epistles because the gospels get to the heart of the message which is Jesus.

The term *gospel* is interesting. It comes from *godspel,* an Old English word for "good news." This word translates the Greek word *euangelion.* From this Greek word we get the words *evangelist* which means "one who proclaims the good news" and *evangelism* which means "the act of proclaiming the good news."

What precisely is the good news which is proclaimed? The New Testament uses *gospel* three ways, ways which echo the three stages of growth of the New Testament discussed in Chapter 1.

1. ***The historical Jesus.*** In his own lifetime Jesus proclaimed the gospel, the good news of God's kingdom. Mark's summary statement of Jesus' mission states it well:

   > "The time has come" he said "and the kingdom of God is close at hand. Repent, and believe the Good News" (Mk 1:15; see also Mt 11:5).

2. ***Oral preaching.*** The early church preached Jesus as the good news of God's love for us. Early Christians burned with the desire to share the good news that Jesus was the Messiah and the Son of God, the long-awaited promised one. St. Paul exemplified this preaching in his sermon to the Jews shortly after his conversion:

   > "We have come to tell you the Good News. It was to our ancestors that God made the promise but it is to us, their children, that he has fulfilled it, by raising Jesus from the dead" (Acts 13:32-33).

3. ***The written gospels.*** Finally, we have the written gospels, that is, four versions of the same gospel, but written through the unique vantage point of four men. For example, the gospel *according to* Mark is the faith witness of Mark who reflected on what God had done in and through Jesus. His unique view of the good news of Jesus was written down for a particular faith community. It was preserved by the church because it presents an important and always fresh witness to Jesus Christ.

This chapter, along with the next three, will pay special attention to the unique insights offered by each of the gospel writers. Keep in mind that our study of the gospels (and the rest of the New Testament as well) is worth our effort because these books help us contact the risen Lord. In this chapter, we will discuss the following:

- the synoptic gospels
- authorship, date and outline of Mark
- a theological overview of the gospel of Mark

GOOD NEWS / BAD NEWS

The gospels are about the good news of Jesus and what he means for us in our relationship to God. Our lives, however, are filled with both good news and bad news. Here are some examples:

Good News	*Bad News*
• You passed a test.	• But you got the lowest grade in the class.
• A friend accepted your invitation to go to the movies.	• But he got sick an hour before the movie began.
• You caught a touchdown pass.	• But the team lost the game.
• You won a citizenship award for helping at the scene of an accident.	• But the newspaper spelled your name wrong.
• God loves you with no strings attached.	• Your acne is acting up again.

Part 1: Add at least four things to each list. Make your examples very personal.

6. ____________________	6. ____________________
____________________	____________________
7. ____________________	7. ____________________
____________________	____________________
8. ____________________	8. ____________________
____________________	____________________
9. ____________________	9. ____________________
____________________	____________________

Part 2: Discuss.

a. Share some of your news with another.

b. What makes good news good? Is it because what happened was planned? unexpected? pleasant? joyful?

c. What do you think is the good in the news about Jesus? How is it good for you personally?

d. Is the good news about Jesus really news? Why or why not? Comment on this quote by G. K. Chesterton:

> "The Christian ideal," it is said, "has not been tried and found wanting; it has been found difficult and left untried."

Why is the good news still newsworthy today?

GOSPEL SYMBOLS

Christians like to make symbols to represent their beliefs. For example, each of the writers of the gospels has been given his own symbol. All four symbols have their source in Ezekiel 1:8-11.

Matthew is depicted as a *man* because he begins his gospel by relating the genealogy of Jesus. There the emphasis is on the humanity of Jesus; hence, the designation of the evangelist by a human figure.

Mark begins his gospel by telling of John the Baptist: "A voice cries in the wilderness." Since a *lion* is heard in the wilds, the lion was taken to symbolize Mark.

Luke is depicted by an *ox* because his gospel begins with the story of Zachary, a priest. As a priest, he offered the customary sacrifice in the Temple: an ox. The theme of sacrifice also appears in Luke's portrayal of Jesus' death.

John's gospel emphasizes the divinity of Christ. His portrayal of Jesus is both lofty and sublime, like the *eagle* who soars gracefully close to the heavens.

SYNOPTIC GOSPELS

The phrase *synoptic gospels* was used earlier in this book to refer to Matthew, Mark and Luke. It means that these gospels can be "looked at together" (you might recognize the root word *optic* as having to do with the eyes). Recall that an aid in studying the synoptics is a book like *Gospel Parallels* which lines up these three gospels in parallel columns so that they can be studied comparatively.

Trying to explain the similarities and differences in these three gospels is called the synoptic problem. Almost all scholars today begin their explanation of this issue by concurring that Mark was the first of the gospels to be written. They reach this conclusion after observing two things: First, almost all the material in Mark's gospel appears in the other two. Scripture scholar William Barclay has noted that there are a total of 661 verses in Mark's gospel. Matthew reproduced 606 of these while Luke used 320 of them. Of the 661 verses, there are only 31 which appear in neither Matthew nor Luke. Second, all three of these gospels follow the same general order of events in retelling the Jesus story. Sometimes Matthew and Luke might vary the order, but one or the other always follows the pattern of Mark in reporting the events of Jesus' life.

How did Mark and the other synoptics come to be? As we saw in Chapter 1, the gospel writers relied on the oral tradition which was preached after Jesus' resurrection. Mark was no exception. He drew on a number of sources to write his gospel: lists of sayings, deeds and miracles of Jesus, parables, faith summaries, prayers and hymns recited at early liturgies, and the like. Additionally, one of Mark's major sources was a fairly detailed account of Jesus' passion and death. Finally, Mark probably had at his disposal the preaching of Peter. Papias, a leading Christian bishop who wrote in the second century, testified that Mark was Peter's interpreter and secretary and that Mark's gospel was an account of Peter's preaching.

Matthew and Luke wrote their gospels sometime after Mark. Their major source was Mark's gospel. They also used a common source of materials *not* used by Mark. It has been designated *Q* which abbreviates the German word *Quelle* meaning "source." Matthew also used material of his own which appears in neither Mark nor Luke. Scholars guess that he had a separate source in the oral tradition which they designate "M" (to refer to a source known to Matthew alone). Luke had a similar body of material which is designated "L." Here is a partial list of passages which come from "M" and "L." These are contained *only* in Matthew or *only* in Luke and do not appear in Mark (or John).

	"M"		"L"
2:1-12	Coming of the wise men	2:1-20	Story of the shepherds
13:24-30	Parable of the Weeds	2:41-52	Jesus at age 12
14:28-33	Peter walking on water	10:29-37	Parable of the Good Samaritan
25:1-13	Parable of the Ten Virgins	19:1-10	Zacchaeus story

To see the relationship among these three gospels better, study the following diagram:

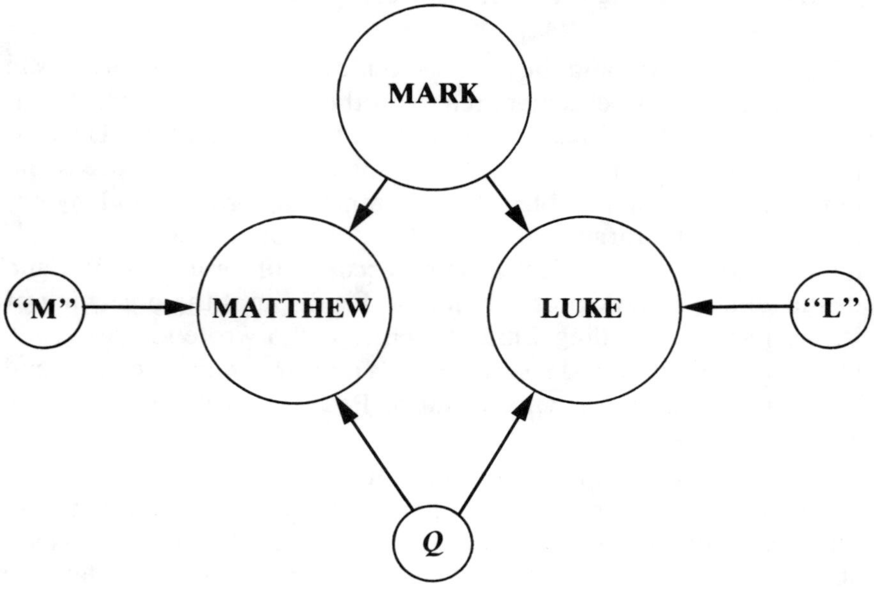

A SYNOPTIC STUDY

Mark's gospel was the earliest written. He also had the most frank, down-to-earth style of all the gospel writers. This style was both simple and direct. It was so direct, in fact, that Matthew and Luke felt they had to soften it at times. Mark tended to state his facts baldly, without lessening their effect. This tendency sometimes made either Jesus or his disciples not "look their best." Discover the directness of Mark's style for yourself. Read the following passages and answer the questions given:

1. *Read Mark 3:20-22.*
   a. What striking charge is brought against Jesus in his own town?
   b. Why might Luke and Matthew have dropped this passage from their gospels?
2. *Read Mark 6:1-6 and Matthew 13:53-58.*
   a. What significant change does Matthew make in v. 58 (compared to Mark's v. 5)?
   b. Try to explain Mark's version. In other words, why *could not* Jesus perform miracles?
3. *Read Mark 10:17-18, Matthew 19:16-17, and Luke 18:18-19.*
   a. Who follows the Marcan account more closely?
   b. Why was the change made?
4. *Read Mark 11:12-14, Matthew 21:18-22, and Luke 13:6-9.*
   a. Who makes the major change from the Marcan version in this account?
   b. Why?

AUTHORSHIP, DATE, OUTLINE OF MARK

The Author

First-century Christians who read the gospels probably did not know who the authors were. Unlike writers of most other kinds of literature, the evangelists stayed in the background as they testified to the good news. It is only from the second century that we get some indication of who is the author of the earliest gospel.

As we have seen above, around the year 140 the Christian bishop Papias attributed authorship of this gospel to Mark, the interpreter and secretary of Peter. More accurately, the author was one John

Mark, a Jew from the Greek-speaking world. John was his Jewish name; Mark was his assumed Greek name.

Mark is referred to several times in Acts and some epistles. They tell us that Mark's mother was Mary, a leading Christian in Jerusalem who used her house for early Christian liturgies (Acts 12:12). His cousin was Barnabas (Col 4:10) whom he accompanied on St. Paul's first missionary journey. Mark was an assistant on that journey, but later deserted it much to Paul's extreme unhappiness (Acts 15:39). One of the final references to Mark is St. Peter calling him affectionately "my son" (1 Pt 5:13). This reference is important in substantiating Papias' claim that Mark served Peter. This early gospel becomes even more meaningful knowing that it may well have been written by an associate of both Paul and Peter.

READING ABOUT MARK

Paul was quite angry with Mark for leaving the first missionary journey. To find out how his attitude to Mark changed, read Philemon 24, Colossians 4:10 and 2 Timothy 4:11.

The Date

For a long time most scholars dated Mark's gospel shortly after the Roman Emperor Nero persecuted the Christians in 64. You may

recall the story of Nero fiddling while the city of Rome burned. The citizens were angry with Nero, who was probably responsible for the fire, so he found a scapegoat in the Christians. Tradition maintains that Peter died by crucifixion that year and that his secretary—Mark—wrote down the essence of his preaching shortly thereafter. Early tradition also held that Mark's gospel was written for a group of Gentile Christians, probably Romans. Mark stressed that disciples of Jesus need to be ready to suffer as Jesus did.

Today several leading scholars hold that Mark's gospel was written shortly after the destruction of the Jewish Temple by Titus in 70. They look to chapter 13 in Mark's gospel to fix a date. This chapter includes Jesus' prediction of the destruction of the Temple. By reading between the lines, these scholars conclude that this event had already taken place by the time Mark wrote his gospel. They also conclude that Mark may have written not for a group of Roman Christians but for a community in Syria, not too far from Jerusalem.

Outline of Mark

As an aid to reading Mark and understanding his theological point of view, here is a brief outline of his gospel.

Prelude: 1:1-13

Part 1: Who Is the Messiah? 1:14-8:26

A. Jesus begins his ministry. He is welcomed but also challenged. 1:14-3:6

B. Jesus spends time in his own country. 3:7-6:6a

C. The meaning of discipleship and mission. 6:6b-8:26

Transition: Jesus = Messiah = Son of Man = Suffering Servant 8:27-8:33

Part 2: Who Is the Son of Man? 8:31-16:8

A. The Son of Man is to suffer. 8:31-10:52

B. Jesus in Jerusalem. 11:1-13:37

C. Passion, death, resurrection. 14:1-16:8

Second Ending of Mark: 16:9-20

KEY READING EXERCISE

Introduction: Before reading any further in this chapter, *it is essential* that you—along with your classmates—complete the following reading and research exercise. This assignment will make you familiar with the themes of Mark's gospel and the outline of the gospel up to the passion and resurrection.

Exercise: An overview of the gospel of Mark

Step 1: Read the Prelude: 1:1-13.

Step 2: Divide into five groups. Each group is responsible for reading and reporting on a particular section of Mark's gospel:

Group 1: Jesus begins his ministry—1:14-3:6

Group 2: Jesus in his own country—3:7-6:6a

Group 3: Meaning of discipleship and mission—6:6b-8:33

Group 4: Son of Man and suffering—8:31-10:52

Group 5: Jesus in Jerusalem—11:1-13:37

Step 3: As a group, prepare a report for your classmates. Chapter-by-chapter, tell your fellow students:

Each major event that took place:

Where this event took place:

Your group's reaction to this event and to the person of Jesus:

THEOLOGY OF MARK'S GOSPEL

This section of the chapter will touch on the major issues of Mark's gospel. To enable you to see how some of these issues fit together, please read the passages cited.

The Prelude (Read 1:1-13)

Mark's introductory verses give a bird's-eye view of two of the main themes which will be raised in his gospel. The first theme deals with Jesus' identity. Who exactly is Jesus? For Mark there is no question about who Jesus is. He forcefully states that Jesus is the Son of God (1:1). This key faith statement is an apt prologue to his gospel. Some of those who met Jesus may have been confused over his identity, but for the reader there is no doubt.

In short order Mark shows how Jesus was baptized by John who came into the wilderness to announce repentance. Significantly, at the baptism Jesus' identity is once again revealed: "You are my Son, the Beloved; my favor rests on you" (1:11). Mark then recalls Jesus' temptation and concludes the Prelude with Jesus rejecting Satan and emerging from the desert with the clear mission of preaching God's kingdom. This rapid summary of the temptation of Jesus and the beginning of his ministry points to a second major theme in Mark's gospel: Knowing who he is, Jesus refuses to be tempted away from his mission of preaching and living the good news. His decision to be faithful to God will eventually lead him to Calvary. After our brief exercise, let us take a closer look at these two themes.

NATURE OF JESUS' TEMPTATIONS

Mark does not give any details of Jesus' temptation in the desert. Both Matthew (4:1-11) and Luke (4:1-13) do, however. Read one of these accounts and fill in the following information. The meaning of these temptations will be explained in the next section of the chapter.

	What is the temptation?	*What is Jesus' response?*
Temptation 1:	____________	____________
	____________	____________
	____________	____________
Temptation 2:	____________	____________
	____________	____________
	____________	____________
Temptation 3:	____________	____________
	____________	____________
	____________	____________

THEME 1: Who Is the Messiah? (Read 1:21-28, 32-34, 40-45; 3:7-12; 5:21-43; 7:31-37 and 8:22-33)

Messianic secret. Did you notice anything peculiar about some of the verses you read? It may have struck you as somewhat strange that after performing a miracle, for example, Jesus would often tell the healed person and other witnesses not to say anything about it to anyone. Certainly if Jesus came to preach the good news it seems somewhat odd that he would not want anyone to know about the deeds he performed. This phenomenon of secrecy in Mark's gospel is sometimes known as the messianic secret.

How can we make sense out of some of these passages and the "secret"? We should note that in this first part of the gospel something marvelous is taking place because of this Jesus. He causes both conflict and confusion. He heals lepers, paralytics, the deformed, the deaf. He calms storms, walks on water, and multiplies loaves. He tells stories that people have difficulty understanding. He argues with the Pharisees over his association with sinners, over his disciples' picking corn on the Sabbath, over some of the harmful traditions of his opponents. He casts out demons. In almost every case, what Jesus says and does causes confusion and outrage.

The key verses in Mark's entire gospel have to be 8:27-33. They hold the key to unlocking the mystery of the messianic secret. Look first at 8:27-30. There Jesus asked the apostles what opinion people had of him. Some thought he was John the Baptist come back to life; in fact, this was the opinion of Herod Antipas. Others thought he was Elijah or one of the other great prophets. But Jesus was even more interested in what the apostles thought. "But you, who do you say I am?" Speaking on behalf of the apostles, Peter responded: "You are the Christ."

Jesus accepted the title. He was indeed the Christ, the promised "anointed one" of Yahweh. But note what happened next in 8:31-33. Jesus began to instruct the apostles on what he meant by *Christ*. He said the Son of Man would suffer terribly, be rejected by the leaders, be put to death and rise after three days. Peter simply could not accept this. After all, was not the Messiah (the Christ) to be a great king, a respected prophet and a holy man honored and recognized by all? How could it be that Jesus would suffer, be rejected and killed? Jesus' words did not make sense. So Peter took Jesus aside and protested against Jesus' interpretation of messiahship.

Jesus had to respond to Peter both forcefully and dramatically. In front of the apostles Jesus likened Peter to Satan who tempted Jesus in the desert. In effect, Jesus was saying something like this: "No, Peter, you are judging by the wrong standards. You are like the devil who tempted me to be the wrong kind of Messiah. He wanted me to turn stones into bread because the people expected the Messiah to do this particular miracle. Satan wanted me to perform a spectacular deed like leaping off a parapet and pulling off a fantastic rescue so that people would believe in me. He begged me to worship him and become the political king of the world. But, Peter, I reject all these interpretations of what it means to be Christ. I am not what people are expecting. I will not force people to believe in me. I am not a political Messiah. Rather, I am doing my Father's will. I have come to serve, not be served. And this will lead to my rejection and death but also to my eventual glorification."

Herein lies the explanation of the messianic secret. Jesus was the Messiah, the Christ. But his version of messiahship was to be a suffering servant. Perhaps he was reluctant to let people spread the word about his deeds because he wanted people to approach him out of true faith. He did not want to be perceived as a magician or a political king. He wanted people, and especially his disciples, to know that the Messiah was to be a suffering servant.

WHO IS JESUS?

Here are some verses about Jesus from Mark's gospel. Decide *who* is responsible for the particular saying. Also see if you can find out *where* the saying took place. Finally, judge if the saying supports(*s*) Jesus' concept of messiahship. If it does, check (✓) the space in Column S. If the saying doesn't support Jesus' concept, then leave the space blank. You might also wish to jot down a key word or two to help you remember what was said about Jesus.

Verse	(Key Words)	Who	Where	S
2:7				
2:16				
3:11				
3:22				
4:41				
5:20				
6:2				
6:14				
6:51				

WHO ARE YOU?

Jesus wanted his friends to understand him properly. Each of us wants to be understood too. Here is a list of descriptions which might tell others who you are. Check (✓) four that *best* describe you. Add to the list if you want.

______ a good student	______ fun-loving
______ a hard worker	______ outgoing
______ a loyal son/daughter	______ shy
______ a faithful friend	______ helpful
______ mechanically inclined	______ artistic
______ a "brain"	______ ______________
______ athletic	______ ______________
______ musical	______ ______________
______ religious	______ ______________

1. Which of these would your father check? your best friend? a classmate? Why might they choose this way?
2. How much does your image of yourself influence your actions? Do other people's images of you affect your actions? How?
3. Is it difficult for you to be different from what people want you to be? Explain. Was this rule true for Jesus, too?

____

THEME 2: Who Is the Son of Man?

Call to Discipleship. The second part of Mark's gospel begins with an instruction to the people and the disciples. Recall that Jesus had just taught that he was the Messiah who was to suffer and die. Furthermore, Jesus rejected any attempt to make him anything else. With this done, he then proceeded to tell his followers what this means for them:

> "If anyone wants to be a follower of mine, let him renounce himself and take up his cross and follow me. For anyone who wants to save his life will lose it; but anyone who loses his life for my sake, and for the sake of the gospel, will save it" (Mk 8:34-35).

The message is clear: *The followers of Jesus must be prepared to suffer as Jesus himself will suffer.* When Christians attempt to live their convictions in an unconvinced world, they must be willing to follow the way of Jesus.

Jesus repeats this same message two other times. He predicts his death (9:32 and 10:35), but once again is misunderstood by his apostles. The first time the apostles argue over who is the greatest among them. Jesus has to remind them that the first among them should become like a servant to others (9:33-37). The second time James and John, the sons of Zebedee, ask for places of honor when Jesus establishes his kingdom. Jesus has to remind them that they should be prepared to suffer with him (10:35-40).

The apostles remain confused and misunderstand Jesus to the very end. One of them—Judas—betrays Jesus. Another—Peter, who confessed Jesus as the Messiah—denies him. Betrayal and denial, perhaps, were temptations for the community for whom Mark wrote. Scholars tell us that Mark probably wrote for a group of Christians who were undergoing persecution. These Christians needed to be reminded that following Jesus meant that they had to be willing to suffer as he did. Mark organized his material to drive home this theme—a theme which would mean very much to the readers and hearers of his gospel.

The Passion (read 14:1-15:47). The whole of Mark's gospel builds up to the passion, death and resurrection of Jesus. The passion narratives were probably the oldest stories circulating in the Christian communities. There is agreement among the four gospels in the story's essentials. In his typical blunt way, Mark does not save the reader from any of the more horrible details. He stresses that Jesus is the Son of Man who came to suffer. The passion story is the climax of that message. Mark also highlights the need for those who follow Jesus to walk in his footsteps. The passion and death show just what those footsteps are. Let us not forget, though, that the good news is really good. Jesus' death leads to a resurrected, glorified life with the Father. Likewise, Christians who walk with Jesus will abide with him and his Father as a reward for being faithful servants.

Outline of the Passion. The story of Jesus' passion and death is an extremely important part of the Christian message. Here is an outline of that story. Some notes are provided to help you understand the story better. You may wish to jot a few notes for yourself, especially for those verses that mean a lot to you.

1. *Chief priests plot against Jesus* (14:1-2). They wanted to put him to death in a way that would not cause an uprising.

2. *Jesus is anointed at Bethany* (14:3-9). The woman who anointed Jesus was doing a good deed in that she was preparing Jesus for his burial. To the Jews, anointing a body for burial was considered better than giving money to the poor.

3. *Judas betrays Jesus* (14:10-11). Mark says Judas plotted with the chief priests for money.

4. *Preparations for Passover Supper* (14:12-16). Jesus planned his last meal in the context of the Passover feast. The man carrying water would have been an unusual sight since this was normally the task of a woman. He would have been easily recognized by the disciples.

5. *The Last Supper* (14:17-31). Jesus foretold his betrayal and once again there was confusion among the apostles. He also predicted Peter's denial. Following Jesus is difficult and may lead to betrayal and denial. Peter is a saint, though, because he never forgot Jesus' forgiveness. Recall, too, that at this Last Supper, Jesus instituted the Eucharist.

6. *Gethsemane* (14:32-52). In his humanity, Jesus did not want to die. He feared death, as any normal person would. But he prayed that the will of his *Abba* be done. The apostles, overcome with fear, could not even stay awake to comfort Jesus. Judas betrayed Jesus at night with a kiss. The arrest took place at night—the hour of Satan—so that the crowds would not come to defend Jesus. Jesus refused to use violence and rejected any temptation to become a political Messiah—the wish of the Zealots. The young man may well have been Mark himself since his mother Mary may have owned the olive grove (*Gethsemane* means "olive press"). This detail has the ring of an eyewitness account.

7. *Jesus before the Sanhedrin* (14:53-72). It was against Jewish law to have a trial at night. The chief priests and Sanhedrin,

the ruling body of the Jews, were trying to frame Jesus by bringing in false witnesses. Jesus admitted that he is the Christ, the Son of God. This claim was blasphemous to the leaders of the Jews and worthy of death. They began to mock Jesus. Peter is recognized as a follower of Jesus because of his Galilean accent. In Jerusalem, someone from the northern region of Israel would have been considered a hick.

8. *Jesus and Pilate* (15:1-20). Only the Romans could exercise capital punishment, so the Jewish leaders had to come up with a charge which would merit death under Roman law. They claimed Jesus was a king who was a rival to Caesar. This was a charge of treason. Jesus was, ironically, the king of the Jews—and of all people. Pilate knew Jesus was innocent but freed instead a known killer, Barabbas. Pilate passed judgment and Jesus was then mocked and beaten by the Roman soldiers.

9. *Crucifixion* (15:21-47). Jesus refused the wine mixed with myrrh because he wanted to feel the full effect of his suffering for us. Crucifixion was a particularly painful way to die. The condemned person usually died of dehydration and asphyxiation. The body, when sufficiently weak, would sag on the cross so that the criminal's diaphragm muscles would not have the strength to exhale air.

   Jesus was mocked and again tempted. This time the temptation was to perform a spectacular deed of rescue.

   Jesus recited aloud the beginning of Psalm 22: "My God, my God, why have you deserted me?" This sounds like a cry of despair, but the psalm ends with a prayer of trust in the mercy of God.

   When Jesus died, the Gentile centurion called Jesus a Son of God.

   The true disciples of Jesus included some women who

remained with him to the end. Joseph of Arimathaea, a member of the Sanhedrin but a disciple of Jesus, buried his Lord. Before releasing the body, however, Pilate made sure Jesus was dead. Jesus died relatively quickly because he was horribly beaten before he was crucified.

10. *Resurrection* (16). Mark's gospel ends with the resurrection of Jesus. Jesus rose as he promised he would. Mark 16:9-20 may have been added to later editions of Mark's gospel. It records some of the appearances listed in other gospels: to Mary Magdalene, to two disciples outside the city, and to the apostles in Jerusalem.

EXERCISES

A. *Passion narratives.* Read the passion narratives in Matthew (26-27) or Luke (22-24). Find at least eight differences between Mark and the other version you read. List them here.

1. ____________________ 5. ____________________

2. ____________________ 6. ____________________

3. ____________________ 7. ____________________

4. ____________________ 8. ____________________

B. *Seven last words of Jesus.* You can tell a lot about people by the way they die. The four passion narratives record seven sayings of Jesus as he hung on the cross. Here they are. As a class, discuss what their significance might be. Then commit them to memory.

Seven last words	*Meaning*
1. *"Father, forgive them; they do not know what they are doing"* (Lk 23:34).	____________________
	____________________
	____________________
	____________________
	____________________

2. *"Indeed, I promise you, today you will be with me in paradise"* (Lk 23:43).

3. *"Woman, this is your son. This is your mother"* (Jn 19:26-27).

4. *"I am thirsty"* (Jn 19:28).

5. *"My God, my God, why have you deserted me?"* (Mk 15:34, Mt 27:46).

6. *"It is accomplished"* (Jn 19:28). ______________________________

____

____

____

____

7. *"Father, into your hands I commit my Spirit"* (Lk 23:46) ______________________________

____

____

____

____

C. *Two Research Topics*

1. How did crucifixion take place in the Roman world?
2. What is the Shroud of Turin?

Sources:

Bible dictionary

Catholic encyclopedia

Recent articles on the shroud

Books, for example,

Bishop, Jim, *The Day Christ Died* (New York: Harper & Row Publishers, 1977).

Barbet, Pierre, *A Doctor at Calvary* (Garden City, New York: Image Books, 1963).

Gorman, C.P., Ralph, *The Trial of Christ* (Huntington, Indiana: Our Sunday Visitor Press, 1972).

D. *Following Christ.* Mark's gospel applies to us as much as it did to suffering Christians in the first century. His message is that we must be willing to walk with Jesus if we wish to be his disciples. Walking with Jesus means standing up for what is right. Examine your degree of discipleship. Where are you on the road to following Jesus? Read the following statements and check the appropriate column.

	This describes me pretty well.	I'm on my way but still need improvement.	I don't know about this one.
1. I tell the truth.			
2. I am honest on exams.			
3. I worship every Sunday.			
4. I pray every day.			
5. I go out of my way to help a lonely class-mate.			
6. I help out at home on a regular basis.			
7. I respect my parents.			
8. I do something extra for the poor.			
9. I occasionally deny myself something for others.			
10. I look on others not as sex objects but as persons.			
11. I watch how I use the Lord's name.			

Add three statements which *you* think are essential for discipleship. Rate yourself.	This describes me pretty well.	I'm on my way but still need improvement.	I don't know about this one.
12.			
13.			
14.			

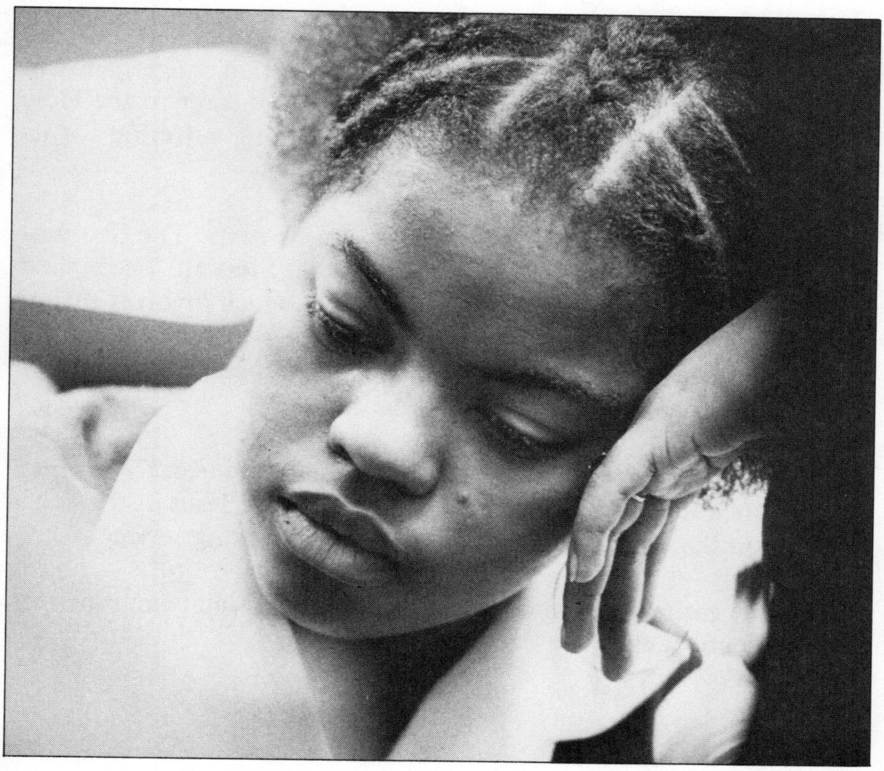

SUMMARY

1. The word *gospel* refers to the good news Jesus preached about God's kingdom. It also refers to Jesus himself and to the written gospels.

2. Mark was the first gospel written. Matthew and Luke used Mark's gospel as a primary source. They also used a common source designated *Q* and their own materials labelled "M" and "L," respectively. These three gospels can be read together and are called the synoptic gospels.

3. Mark's style of writing is down-to-earth, simple and direct.

4. Papias attributes Mark's gospel to the secretary and interpreter of Peter, a man by the name of John Mark.

5. Mark wrote his gospel between 65 and 70. There is some debate as to whether he wrote for a Gentile-Christian congregation in Rome or for a Christian community somewhere nearer to the Holy Land. In any case the community was undergoing suffering for its faith.

6. Mark's gospel is divided into two major parts. The first part deals with the true identity of Jesus as a servant Messiah. The second part treats the theme of Christian discipleship which involves suffering for the Lord. The entire gospel up to chapter 14 can be seen as a prelude to the passion narratives which play a crucial role in Mark's version of the good news.

7. The key verses in Mark's gospel can be found in 8:27-33 where Peter confesses that Jesus is the Messiah and where Jesus instructs his apostles on the true nature of messiahship—suffering service.

8. The earliest stories circulating in the Christian community of the first century were the passion narratives.

EVALUATION

1. From what Old English word is the term *gospel* derived?

____

2. The symbol for the evangelist Mark is a. an ox; b. a man; c. a lion; d. an eagle.

3. Identify *Q*: ________________________________

4. John Mark was a cousin to a. Paul; b. Barnabas; c. Peter; d. James.

____

5. List three titles Mark attributes to Jesus:

______________ ______________ ______________

6. What is meant by the messianic secret?

____

7. According to Mark, the true disciple of Jesus must be willing to

____

8. When and where did Jesus institute the sacrament of the Eucharist?

____

9. What was the Sanhedrin?

____

10. List the seven last words of Jesus.

a. ____________________ e. ____________________

b. ____________________ f. ____________________

c. ____________________ g. ____________________

d. ____________________

READING GOD'S WORD

St. Luke wrote the Acts of the Apostles, a chronicle of the spread of Christianity from Jerusalem to the very ends of the Roman Empire. The central figure in the spread of the good news in the first century was St. Paul. You read about his conversion in the last chapter.

The reading exercises in the next few chapters will trace this spread of Christianity. You'll be reading about the various missionary journeys of St. Paul. There were three of them. A final journey took him to Rome where he was put under house arrest for a period of time.

It is fitting in this chapter to begin with Paul's first missionary journey because John Mark (the reputed author of Mark's gospel) accompanied him and his cousin Barnabas on it (Acts 12:25).

Read Acts 13-14.

After you've read the assigned chapters, answer the comprehension questions given below. Then trace Paul's journey on the map reproduced on page 101. Use a dotted line (. . . . .) to represent Paul's first journey. You'll be using this same map to trace Paul's two other journeys.

13:4-12 What happened to Elymas Magos and why?

____

13:14-16: When he got to the cities, where did Paul first go to preach?

____

13:44-52: What kind of reaction did Paul and Barnabas get from the Jews and what did they do as a result of this reaction?

____

14:1-7: Why did the apostles flee Iconium?

____

14:8-18: What happened in the region of Lycaonia?

____

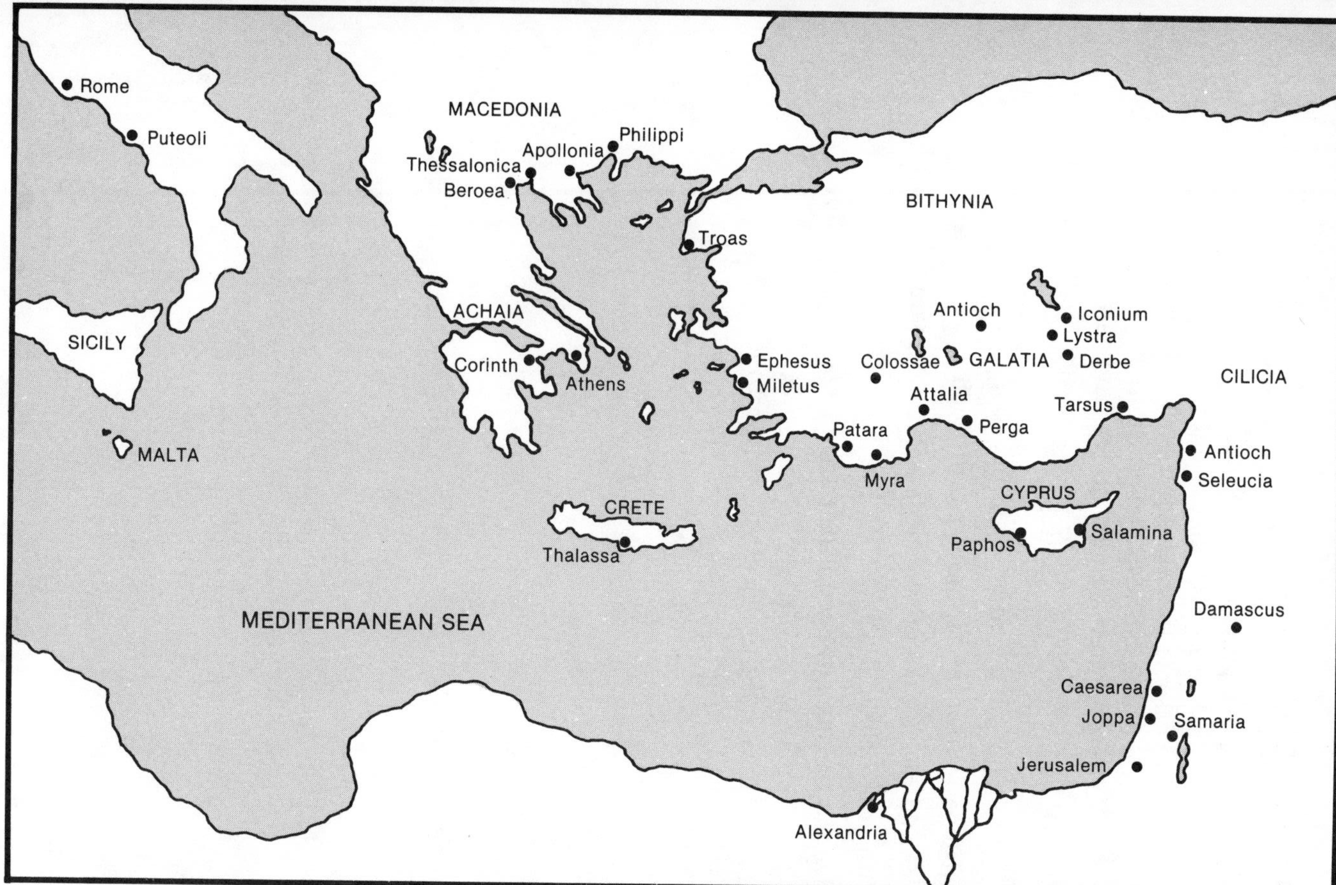

Paul's Missionary Journeys: 1st journey .... 2nd journey _ _ _ _ 3rd journey ________

PRAYER REFLECTION

Oh Lord, you ask great things of me.
You ask me to be honest and true.
You ask me to stand up for what's right.
You ask me to resist temptation.
You ask me to respect others, and care for them, and to go out of my way for them.
You ask me so much more, too.

I wish to follow you. I know it is difficult.

You told me to take up my cross and follow you.

With your help, I'll try.

Give me the strength to do the things I know I must do.

Give me your Spirit to guide me.
Give me true friends to support me.

Thanks, Lord. I'll try. Amen.

4
Gospel of Matthew—Call to Community

Then the King will say to those on his right hand, "Come, you whom my Father has blessed, take for your heritage the kingdom prepared for you since the foundation of the world. For I was hungry and you gave me food; I was thirsty and you gave me drink; I was a stranger and you made me welcome; naked and you clothed me, sick and you visited me, in prison and you came to see me."

—Matthew 25:34-36

This chapter opens with some very important verses from Matthew's gospel. In them Jesus identifies love of God with love of neighbor. We will be judged worthy of everlasting life if we take the time and effort to seek out the lonely, the neglected, the sick and the poor. Matthew's gospel is loaded with insights like this. He writes to Christians and emphasizes that we must live a different kind of life now that we have met Jesus Christ. We are both light of the world and salt of the earth.

This important message from Matthew has not been lost on Christians. Matthew's gospel has been rightly revered in Christian circles as the gospel which challenges the followers of Jesus, the church, to live up to the ideals that Jesus taught and left with us.

Have you ever wondered why, of the four gospels, Matthew's is listed first? One commentator suggests that Matthew appears first because it has been the most frequently used by the church, especially in its long history of liturgical worship. Another commentator suggests that Matthew's gospel heads the list because it is the perfect bridge between the Old and the New Testaments. As we shall see, the author of Matthew quotes the Hebrew scriptures numerous times to try to convince the reader that Jesus is the fulfillment of the prophecies made about the Messiah in the Old Testament.

The best explanation for Matthew's gospel heading the list goes like this: Eusebius, a bishop-historian of the fourth century, quoted Papias as saying that there was an earlier gospel written in Aramaic (the language of Jesus) by an apostle of Jesus, perhaps no more than 15 or 20 years after Jesus' death and resurrection. The Matthew we have today, of course, was written in Greek sometime after Mark's gospel. Matthew, then, leads the list because it was believed that the later Greek version relied on the earlier Aramaic gospel. However, the relationship between the earlier Aramaic Matthew and the later Greek Matthew which we have today is unclear.

This chapter will study the gospel of Matthew by treating the following important areas:

- a look at the stories of Christ's birth
- authorship, date and outline of Matthew
- theological overview of Matthew's gospel
- Sermon on the Mount
- discipleship in the kingdom
- titles of Jesus

TWO THOUGHT-PROVOKERS

A. *You and the Church*. Many scholars have stated that Matthew's gospel is *the* gospel of the church. As a matter of fact, of the four gospel writers only Matthew uses the word church (*ekklesia* in Greek). He does so only twice. The first time refers to the special place of Peter, the "rock" on whom Jesus would build his church (16:18); the second time concerns the need to consult the church if a Christian brother or sister should harm another member (18:15-17).

Here are 10 areas with which the Catholic church is very concerned. Check (✓) the five which you think should hold the most important positions in the life of the church.

______ the Beatitudes	______ word of God (scripture)
______ belief in the Trinity	______ building up Christian community (through teaching)
______ distribution of food to the poor and other works of mercy	______ preaching the word of God to nonbelievers
______ the Eucharist (Mass)	______ leaders (priests)
______ forgiveness of sin (sacrament of reconciliation)	______ laws of the church designed for church order

Discuss:

1. Why did you choose as you did? Compare your list with those of your classmates. Are there any significant differences?
2. Is there any essential item which was left off the list? As a young person, is there anything you think should be added?

B. *Happiness*

Part 1: One of the basic human rights granted by the American Constitution is the right to pursue happiness. What makes you happy? List eight things that you are pursuing or would like to pursue which would make you happy.

1. ______________________	5. ______________________
2. ______________________	6. ______________________
3. ______________________	7. ______________________
4. ______________________	8. ______________________

Discuss:

1. Who is the happiest person you know? Why? What makes a person unhappy?
2. What is happiness?

Part 2: One of the happy things about Matthew's gospel is that it contains the charter for Christian happiness, the eight Beatitudes. Please read them now in Matthew 5:1-12. How happy are you in light of those qualities which our Lord says will bring true happiness? Check the appropriate column.

CHARTER FOR HAPPINESS				
	This describes me well	I'm on my way	I've got a long way to go	I don't know what this means
1. Happy the poor in spirit.				
2. Happy the gentle.				
3. Happy those who mourn.				
4. Happy those who hunger and thirst for what is right.				
5. Happy the merciful.				
6. Happy the pure in heart.				
7. Happy the peace-makers.				
8. Happy those who are persecuted in the cause of right.				

Sharing: Share with your classmates one example of when you did experience true happiness because you manifested one of the virtues listed above.

STORIES OF CHRIST'S BIRTH

Read Matthew 1-2 and Luke 1-2.

The stories about Jesus' birth, called infancy narratives, are among the most memorable in the gospels. Everyone likes hearing about a baby wrapped in swaddling clothes, a baby who is God's gift to us, Jesus his Son. Matthew and Luke alone recount these infancy stories. Why did they write them down?

To answer this question, it might be good to recall how the early Christians preached the risen Lord. As we saw in Chapter 1, early Christian preachers began by announcing the incredible good news that Jesus lived, that he was glorified with his Father and that he could be met in faith through the gift of the Holy Spirit. They went on to tell of Jesus' suffering and death. His words and teachings were remembered and applied to current situations in the Christian community.

Only after many years did the early Christians put together stories about Jesus' birth. These emerged to satisfy the desire of believers to understand better the full meaning of Jesus' saving works and words. The infancy narratives are filled with symbolism which draws out the fuller meaning of Jesus for the believer. Father Raymond Brown, an expert on these infancy narratives, believes that these stories in Matthew and Luke contain an overview of the theology of their respective gospels.

For comparative purposes, let us pause here to outline briefly the major events in the two versions.

MATTHEW	LUKE
• Ancestry of Jesus	• Jesus' and John's births foretold
• Conception of Jesus	• Annunciation
• Born in Bethlehem	• Visitation
• Visit of the Magi	• Magnificat

- Flight into Egypt
- Slaughter of the Innocents
- Return to Nazareth in Galilee

- Birth and circumcision of John
- Benedictus
- Hidden life of John the Baptist
- Birth of Jesus
- Visit of the shepherds
- Presentation in the Temple: Simeon and Anna
- Hidden life of Jesus
- Jesus at 12

How can we explain the differences between Matthew and Luke? Recall from Chapter 1 of this book that the authors had their own theological points to make in writing their gospels. They selected certain details to reinforce their overriding concerns. Let us see how this was done.

Matthew's Version

Matthew wrote for a group of Christians who had at one time been Jews. His main theological concern was to show how Jesus fulfilled the promises made to Israel concerning the Messiah. He did this beautifully in his infancy narratives.

1. Jesus' ancestry can be traced to Abraham. *Jesus is the Messiah,* greater than David, *promised to the Jews.* He is the son of David, son of Abraham.

2. *Jesus is the son of David through the power of the Holy Spirit.* His origin is divine ("God-is-with-us") as well as human and was prophesied in Isaiah:

> The virgin will conceive and give birth to a son and they will call him Emmanuel (Mt 1:23).

Matthew goes on to point out that another son of David, Joseph, accepts the message of the angel about Jesus' divine origin (1:24).

3. *Jesus is born in Bethlehem,* the home of David and the town from which the Messiah would come according to the prophecy of Micah (2:6). He is accepted by the Gentiles as represented by the Magi who recognize that Jesus is special when they give him presents meant for a king—gold, frankincense and myrrh. Here Matthew points to the fact that many of the Jews would fail to accept Jesus and that the glorified Lord would commission his apostles to preach the gospel to all the nations (Mt 28:19).

4. *Jesus is like Moses and the people of Israel.* To escape death, Jesus is taken to Egypt. This recalls Moses' own narrow escape from the pharaoh. Herod then slaughters the innocent children, a slaughter that makes Matthew cite a quote from Jeremiah (see Mt 2:18) and a slaughter that symbolically points to Jesus' own death. Jesus is like Israel in that he is called back from Egypt (Hosea wrote: "I called my son out of Egypt"). He settled in Nazareth in the northern part of the Holy Land which was considered by pious Jews to be "polluted" with Gentiles. It is from this territory that Jesus would embark on his mission of teaching the good news.

Luke's Version

Luke wrote for a group of Gentile Christians. His dominant concern was to show that Jesus was the universal Messiah, the Lord who came to help everyone, even the lowly. This theme will be discussed in more detail in the next chapter.

1. Jesus' and John's stories are interwoven, but notice it is *Jesus who is the Messiah, a Messiah with divine origins.* His mother, Mary, accepts with humble faith the mystery of God's work. John's mother, Elizabeth, testifies to Jesus' origins when Mary visits her. John's father, Zechariah, blesses God's wonderous work in his hymn, "The Benedictus," when he says to his son John:

> And you, little child,
> you shall be called Prophet of the Most High,
> for you will go before the Lord
> to prepare the way for him (Lk 1:76).

The angels sing their song of praise to the Messiah and the prophets Simeon and Anna bless God for being allowed to see him.

2. *Jesus comes first to the lowly.* Jesus was born in the poorest of circumstances. The shepherds see him first. They were considered unholy by the pious Jews because their occupation did not allow them to practice all the religious rituals demanded by the Jewish religion. Yet Jesus manifested himself to them first. He is the Messiah of the simple folk, the outcast, even the old like Simeon and Anna.

3. *For Luke, Jerusalem plays a key role.* Jesus journeys there to die, but the early Christians, empowered by the Holy Spirit, go from Jerusalem to the ends of the world to preach Jesus as Lord. As Luke's gospel opens, Zechariah is in Jerusalem. Jesus is presented in the Temple there and at the age of 12 even travels to Jerusalem from Nazareth. Jesus' time there points to the future when he will again confound the learned, some of whom will then plot for his death.

YOUR CHRISTIAN ROOTS

What is the story of your origins? You might wish to find an answer to these questions.

1. *Your Christian name.* Jesus' name means "Yahweh saves." Luke saw that Jesus' name was *not* given to him accidentally (see Lk 1:31).

   a. What is your Christian name? ____________________

   b. What does it mean? ____________________

   c. Why did your parents give you this name? ____________________

   ____

   d. Does your name have any special symbolism for you?

   ____

2. *Your surname.* Jesus' surname would have been one of these three: (1) Jesus, *son of Joseph*; (2) Jesus *the Carpenter*; (3) Jesus *the Nazarene.* Check with a parent or a grandparent to see if you can discover the meaning of your surname. If so, write it here:

   ____

3. *Christian birth.* For Christians, real birth takes place at baptism. Discover the answers to these questions:

   a. Where were you baptized (city and church)?

   ____

   b. When were you baptized? ____________________

   c. Who were your godparents? Do you ever see them?

   ____

   ____

4. *Your story.* Discover from your family what took place on the day you were born. What do they remember about the day? Perhaps you could read a newspaper from your birthdate. Your local library may have it on microfilm. List some key events of that day here:

   ____

   ____

   ____

   Share your "nativity story" with a classmate.

____

AUTHORSHIP, DATE, OUTLINE OF MATTHEW

The Author

Ancient tradition taught that the apostle Matthew wrote the gospel named after him. This tradition is based on the belief that there was an earlier version of the gospel written in Aramaic between A.D. 40-45, the so-called Hebrew gospel. If it existed, this Aramaic gospel was lost some time in the first century. The gospel we have today is written in Greek for a community of Jewish Christians who spoke that language. It may or may not have been based on the earlier Aramaic gospel. Several New Testament commentators believe that if it was based on the earlier work, the Greek gospel has been substantially reworked. Authorship of the Greek Matthew is attributed to an anonymous Jewish scribe or rabbi.

The author of Matthew assumes that his audience has a familiarity with Jewish customs. For example, he uses terms like *Preparation Day, Gehenna* (the Jewish term for "hell") and *Beelzebul* (a Hebrew name for "the devil"). He refers to Jewish customs such as the ritual washing of hands before eating and the wearing of phylacteries.* In none of these cases does he explain his terms.

Furthermore, two of the major themes of the gospel would have been burning concerns for a former Jew. First, the author is very interested in showing the relationship between the old Law and Jesus' Law of Love. Second, he is quite concerned with the fate of Israel which had, by and large, rejected the Messiah.

READING ABOUT MATTHEW

Some scholars suggest that the author of Matthew's gospel may have been a former Jewish scribe. They conclude this by noting what the author of Matthew has done in several cases when he borrowed his material from Mark. See this for yourself. Read Mark 14:43, then Matthew 26:47. Answer these two questions:

1. What did Matthew leave out?
2. What is a possible motivation for his doing so?

---

* A *phylactery* was a small leather capsule which was fastened either on the forehead or on the upper left arm so that it hung at the level of the heart. It contained miniature scrolls with four passages from the Jewish Law, all alluding to the need to keep the Law of God before one's eyes and heart. A pious Jewish male—like a Pharisee (Mt 23:5)—would wear these all day once he reached adulthood (age 14).

The Date

Matthew is generally dated between the years 70 and 90. These dates seem reasonable because Matthew used Mark's gospel and, as a result, had to be written sometime after Mark circulated his work. In addition, evidence in Matthew's gospel suggests antagonism between the Pharisees and the followers of Jesus. This may reflect somewhat the antagonism between Jewish Christians and the Jews (Pharisees) of Matthew's day. History tells us, for example, that the Pharisees were greatly upset that the Christians did not fight alongside Jews against the Romans in the revolt of 66-70. As a result, Jews who survived the revolt made it very difficult for Christians to participate in the synagogue services after about 75. These tense relations between Jews and their Christian brothers and sisters may well have influenced some viewpoints expressed by the author of Matthew when he wrote his gospel. These viewpoints, often appearing as sharp sayings against the Pharisees, should *not* be read as a condemnation of either the Jews or the Pharisees as such. Rather, they should be read as reflecting the controversies which were taking place at the time that Matthew's gospel was written.

THE CONTROVERSY

To get a flavor of the controversy raging between the Christians of Matthew's day and the Pharisaic branch of Judaism, read Matthew 23. There Jesus is addressing the people and his *disciples,* telling them what kind of leaders they are supposed to be. The remarks there apply to any Christian who wishes to follow Jesus. After reading Matthew 23, answer these questions:

1. How should a Christian teacher act? ____________________

   ____

2. List three hypocritical things Jesus condemns:

   a. ______________________________________

   b. ______________________________________

   c. ______________________________________

Outline of Matthew's Gospel

Matthew wrote a highly structured gospel. It falls neatly into seven major divisions. The heart of the gospel is the five sections from chapters 3-26. These sections each contain a narrative and a major speech or discourse of Jesus. Each of them ends with a formula that goes something like this: "Jesus had now finished what he wanted to say . . ." (7:28, 11:1, 13:53, 19:1 and 26:1).

For many years scholars thought this fivefold division was intended by the author of Matthew to show that Jesus was like the new Moses. The five sections supposedly corresponded to the Torah, the first five books of the Old Testament.

Today the more popular opinion is that Matthew collected together sayings and teachings of Jesus into a kind of catechism for new believers. Jesus is presented as a supreme teacher who answers questions like these for new Christians: How am I to live as a Christian? What is Christian leadership like? What is God doing in the world? How should the Christian community conduct itself? What is the new age going to be like? Matthew's gospel, then, should be seen as a book of Christian instruction and administration.

Here is the outline:

Chapters

I. Prologue: Birth of the Messiah 1-2

II. Coming of the Kingdom

Narrative: Jesus' commission and the selection of the disciples 3-4

Discourse: Sermon on the Mount 5-7

III. Works of Jesus

Narrative: Ten miracles 8-9

Discourse: Mission of the disciples 10

IV. God's Kingdom

Narrative: Jesus and his opponents 11-12

Discourse: Parables of the kingdom 13

V. The Kingdom Developing

Narrative: Messiah as shepherd of Israel.........14-17

Discourse: Advice to the church................18

VI. Mounting Opposition to Jesus

Narrative: Controversies......................19-22

Discourse: Judgment...........................23-25

VII. Death and Resurrection of Jesus................26-28

TWO READING EXERCISES

A. *Narratives in Matthew.* Divide the class into five groups. Each group should read one of the narrative sections from the outline above. As a group prepare a report for your classmates. Chapter by chapter tell your fellow students:

The major events that take place	*The people who are involved in the story*
______________________	______________________
______________________	______________________
______________________	______________________
______________________	______________________
______________________	______________________
______________________	______________________
______________________	______________________

B. *Jesus and prophecy.* In your reading of the infancy narratives you have already seen how Matthew tries to show that Jesus fulfills Old Testament prophecies. Throughout his gospel Matthew quotes Old Testament prophets, especially Isaiah, concerning the Messiah. Here are some of the references: 4:15-16; 8:17; 12:17-21; 13:14-15; 13:35; 21:5; 27:9. Encircle the ones which describe the coming Messiah. In a few brief words tell what kind of Messiah Jesus is:

____

____

____

THEOLOGICAL OVERVIEW OF MATTHEW'S GOSPEL

Matthew's Jesus is a teacher *par excellence.* You can see this pretty clearly by looking at the outline of the gospel. In five important speeches, Jesus touches on many of the themes which were central to his message and mission. All of these themes are important for followers of Jesus. In this section of the chapter we will look at several of these speeches.

Sermon on the Mount

(Read Mt 5-7)

The first and perhaps most important of Jesus' discourses in Matthew is the famed Sermon on the Mount. Here Matthew collected together a number of Jesus' main teachings on the moral life. It is a classic example of a *didache*, that is, a teaching that is directed to Christians who have already accepted the good news of Jesus. This important sermon makes the point that it is not enough just to believe in Jesus:

> "It is not those who say to me, 'Lord, Lord,' who will enter the kingdom of heaven, but the person who does the will of my Father in heaven" (7:21).

We must change and become loving, treating others the way we would like to be treated (7:12). Let's look more closely at several sections of the Sermon on the Mount to see what Jesus asks of us once we have accepted his good news.

1. *Salt of the earth and light of the world* (5:13-16). Jesus calls us, his followers, both salt and light. Salt has the quality of flavoring food. Like salt, we should live a quality of life which changes the "flavor" of the world. The world should be different because of the way we Christians live. Salt likewise preserves meat; it has a saving function. By the way we live, Christians help keep the world from rotting. By virtue of our Lord's grace and life in us, we should help the world be a better place.

We are also likened to light. Light dispels darkness. But darkness is only overcome if we let our good works shine forth. With both of these images Jesus is exhorting his followers to do the good we must do to make the good news come alive in the world. How is this to be done?

2. *Live a different quality of life* (5:17-6:18). Because we are salt and light, we must live a different kind of life than unbelievers live. Jesus makes this point through a number of teachings. First, he says he is not talking about ignoring the Old Testament Law, for example, the Ten Commandments. We Christians *must* keep the commandments; it is only by living them that we can ever be called great in God's kingdom (5:19).

What we must do is live a different *quality* of life. We are not just to keep the old Law. Rather, we should bring to it an attitude of proper intention. For example, we should not kill, nor should we be angry—that which leads to killing. We are not to commit adultery, nor even lust—that which leads to adultery. We should be faithful to our spouses and not divorce them. We should be truthful in everything we say; for Christians there is no need to swear an oath to back up our word. Above all else, Christians should not seek revenge. We should forgive those who have harmed us and love even our enemies. These difficult commands are made possible by Jesus' life in us. He has given us much and as a result asks for much in return. He calls us to perfection as his Father is perfect. What this means is that we should strive to be more loving and more responsive to others.

Intention is very important for Jesus. We should do our good works not for show but out of love for our Father in heaven. Thus we should give money to the poor, pray, and fast in a way that does not seek the approval of others. God loves us and has already rewarded us. Why should we be motivated by what others think of us?

3. *Trust in the Lord* (6:19-7:29). Jesus exhorts us to put first things first. If his Father takes care of the birds in the sky and the flowers of the field how much more will he take care of us? Furthermore, what's the sense of worrying? Worrying about tomorrow can only cause grief. Jesus teaches that we should put everything in its proper perspective, even money. If we strive to do the right thing, our

Father who only wishes good for us will give us that which is good and necessary for true life, for salvation. The true disciple will take these words to heart and build his life on them. These teachings provide the basis for a solid response to the Lord, a response that cannot be shaken by anything.

Summary. Jesus demands much of his followers. We should be different because we have accepted the good news. But he continually reminds us that he will not forget us. If we pray with forgiveness in our hearts, our Abba—our loving, heavenly Father—will provide for us and take care of our real needs. The Sermon on the Mount is the charter statement of the Christian life. If we want to know what it means to be a disciple of Jesus, we need but look to these magnificent teachings from the greatest of teachers.

FOR REFLECTION AND ACTION

A. *The sermon and you.* How important are the following things to you? Check (✓) those items which you think about on a daily basis.

______ college or a future job	______ popularity at school
______ your relationship with your friends	______ your relationship with members of the opposite sex
______ money and possessions	______ mistakes you've made
______ your relationship with God	

- Look again at the Sermon on the Mount. Find something in the sermon which talks either specifically or generally about these concerns. Share what you found.
- *Discuss:* Is Jesus' teaching realistic for you? Why or why not?

B. *Doing for others.* The Sermon on the Mount assumes that we, as followers of Jesus, will treat others the way we would like to be treated. Perhaps as a class you could undertake a project which would help the sermon come alive. Here are two examples:

- *Almsgiving*—giving money to the poor. Perhaps you can sponsor a car wash or some other event to raise money for a favorite charity. Donate the money anonymously.
- *Fasting.* We fast—stay away from certain foods—not only to "feel for" the poor (that is, *empathize* with them) but to realize that the source of all food, our gifts, even life itself is our Father. Perhaps your class could sponsor a school-wide hunger day to stress both of these themes; for example, suggest that people abstain from junk food for a day or so and donate the cost of these items to a hunger relief agency. The focus of the day would be to remind people of our oneness with the poor and our need to be grateful for the gifts we have been given.

Discipleship and the Kingdom: A Call to Community
(Read Mt 13 and Mt 18)

Two concepts are closely related in Matthew's gospel: kingdom and discipleship. Matthew's is the gospel of the church. In chapter 18 Matthew collects some key sayings about the church. For him the church is the family of God's children. The center of the family is Jesus who is its guide and model. Jesus is present in his church. He rules over it and through it he establishes his kingdom. The kingship of God—his rule of peace and justice—is present in the community of Christians who live God's life. But the kingdom is greater than the church, too. It is the reign of God that will come in its fullest glory in the future.

1. *The kingdom parables* (13). This chapter contains a list of parables where Jesus teaches about his Father's kingdom. He uses vivid examples of sowing seed in good and bad soil, of minute seeds maturing into strong plants, of weeds growing with good crops, of yeast slowly leavening the dough, of finding unexpected treasure in a field, of a marvelous discovery of a pearl, and the like. The message here is quite clear: Despite the meager appearances, God is marvelously bringing a whole new day. God's kingdom is inevitable. It may appear battered and besieged, but his kingdom will triumph!

In the meantime, as the kingship of God spreads in the world, Jesus calls his disciples to a radically different kind of life. These disciples are to band together in a community where they are to love God above all things and the neighbor as self (Mt 22:34-40).

2. *Instructions to the community* (18). Jesus recognized that his followers were a collection of very human men and women. They needed constant reminders to live as worthy members of God's kingdom. Chapter 18 of the gospel reminds members of Jesus' church that the greatest in the kingdom is one who humbles himself or herself like a child. In addition, Christians should not give bad example. They should settle their disputes in ways that befit brothers and sisters. They should pray together and forgive each other, even 77 times! Furthermore, Christian leaders should be models of love and forgiveness, not like the unforgiving debtor in Jesus' parable who refused to forget about a meager sum after being relieved of a 10,000-talent debt (18:23-35).

In summary, followers of Jesus are to bind themselves into a community of love and live under the kingship of a merciful, loving and generous Lord. Christians are to be light which illuminates the wonderful work of God in human history.

A PLEDGE

Many Americans consider the late Martin Luther King Jr. a true follower of Jesus who worked for the establishment of God's kingdom, especially for the victims of discrimination. Reverend King tried to imitate Jesus' own nonviolent life in working for a just society. He asked his followers to commit themselves to the ten commandments of his nonviolent movement. Here are *some* of these statements of commitment. Check (✓) those to which you think you could commit yourself. With your classmates, come up with several examples of how people in your parish could live each of them.

My commitment		*Examples*
______	Meditate daily on the teachings and life of Jesus.	______ ______ ______
______	Remember always that the nonviolent movement seeks justice and reconciliation, not victory.	______ ______ ______
______	Walk and talk in the manner of love, for God is love.	______ ______ ______
______	Sacrifice personal wishes in order that all men might be free.	______ ______ ______ ______ ______

______	Observe, with friend and foe, the ordinary rules of courtesy.	______ ______ ______
______	Seek to perform regular service for others and for the world.	______ ______ ______
______	Restrain from the violence of fist, tongue or heart.	______ ______ ______
______	Strive to be in good spiritual and bodily health.	______ ______ ______

Titles of Jesus in Matthew's Gospel (Read 28:16-20)

The New Testament attributes many titles to Jesus. They tell us what people believed about Jesus both in his lifetime on earth and what Christians believed about Jesus after his resurrection. Each of the gospel writers stresses certain of these titles to reflect his own theological stance to Jesus. We have seen, for example, how important the title Christ was to Mark and how he linked it with Suffering Servant. Listed here with a brief discussion are all of the titles used in Matthew's gospel.

1. *Favorite titles of Matthew*

a. Son of Abraham and Son of David. Only Matthew uses Son of Abraham (1:1). His favorite title is Son of David (used eight times). Both of these titles show Jesus as the fulfillment of the Old Testament promises made to the Jews. Jesus is in the line of David and is the promised Messiah of God.

b. Emmanuel. Emmanuel means "God is with us" (Mt 1:23). Matthew dramatically underscores the fact that in and through Jesus God dwells with his people. This idea is present in a number of places in Matthew's gospel. When Jesus commissions the apostles at the end of the gospel, he promises to be with the Christian community until the end of time. This same idea is present when Jesus says wherever two or three are gathered in his name, he is there in their midst. We believe this means, among other things, that Jesus is present in a special way when we worship in liturgical celebrations.

2. *Titles used by Matthew and the other synoptic gospels*

a. Messiah (Christ). Matthew reproduces Peter's confession of faith in 16:16. Jesus is God's anointed one who will bring salvation. He is not, however, the kind of Messiah expected by many of the Jewish sects of his day.

b. Servant of God. Like Mark, Matthew stresses that Jesus' concept of messiahship was that of Suffering Servant. For example, in several places reference is made to the Suffering Servant songs of Isaiah (Mt 9:15 and 8:17).

c. Lord. In most cases in the synoptics *Lord* is used by the disciples and others in the sense of "Sir" or "Master." In the Acts and Paul's letters, *Lord* is a powerful statement of Jesus' divinity. *Lord* is the translation for the Greek *Kurios* which in turn translates the Hebrew word for Yahweh (God). To call Jesus Lord is to call him God. Matthew uses this title in the fullest sense when he refers to the risen Christ near the end of his gospel (28:6).

d. Rabbi. In his lifetime Jesus was most often addressed by this title or "Master." *Rabbi* means "teacher."

e. Son of Man. Jesus used this title of himself more than any other. In Mark, "Son of Man" appears 14 times, in Matthew 30, in Luke 25 and in John 13.

It means two things: First, it simply refers to humanity; second, to a heavenly figure who will come at the end of time to establish God's kingdom (see Dn 7:13). The gospel writers use it to refer to

Jesus' earthly ministry (for example, Mt 13:37), his suffering and resurrection (Mt 17:22-23), and his function at the end of time (Mt 25:31).

Jesus' use of the title is highly symbolic in that he connects two ideas. Jesus is God's agent who will establish the kingdom, but at the same time he is a human (like us) who will suffer and die for people. This title helps us see what Jesus thought of himself. It blends together the concept of Suffering Servant and Messiah.

A FINAL EXERCISE

Before leaving Matthew's gospel, look again at the theme of church. Based on citations from Matthew and other New Testament sources, here is a profile of what the Christian community should be. Please do the following things:

- Read the references given.

The New Testament on the Church

_____ 1. A community that goes out to all people. (Mt 28:19-20)

_____ 2. A community of believers. (Rom 12:4-8)

_____ 3. A community that reaches out to sinners. (Lk 19:10)

_____ 4. A community founded by Christ on Peter and the apostles. (Mt 16:15-19)

_____ 5. A community that loves as Jesus loved. (Mt 25:31-46)

_____ 6. A community with worship centered on the Eucharist. (1 Cor 10:15-17)

_____ 7. A community that suffers with Christ. (Mt 5:10-12)

_____ 8. A community of faith as taught by the apostles. (Acts 4:1-4, 33)

Should anything be added?

- Analyze your own parish or school community to see if it lives up to the criteria given. Check (✓) each point that does describe your particular Christian community.
- Discuss what must be done to enable either of these two communities to live up to the New Testament requirement. Make concrete suggestions.

SUMMARY

1. Using symbol and story the infancy narratives in Matthew and Luke treat the theological themes of their gospels. Matthew shows how Jesus fulfills the Old Testament prophecies made about him. Luke emphasizes universal messiahship.

2. The author of Matthew's gospel was a former Jew, perhaps a scribe. He wrote his gospel for a Jewish-Christian audience to show Jesus as the fulfillment of the Old Testament.

3. Matthew's gospel was written between 70 and 90. It has seven major divisions with the central five making up the heart of the gospel. Each of these five divisions has a narrative section about Jesus' ministry and a major discourse in which Jesus teaches the good news.

4. The Sermon on the Mount underscores the theme that belief in our Lord implies loving others. Christians are both light and salt. Our Lord demands much of his followers but in return shares his own life with them.

5. In some important parables Matthew's Jesus teaches about the inevitable conquest of God's kingdom. Christians, through their humility, forgiveness, good example and prayer, demonstrate that God's kingdom has come.

6. The titles of Jesus are a key to what the disciples and early Christians believed about him. Son of Abraham, Son of David and Emmanuel are favorite titles used by Matthew. Other important ones include Messiah, Servant of God, Lord, Rabbi and Son of Man.

EVALUATION

Directions: Mark a "T" for any true statement; mark an "F" for any statement which is false.

____ 1. Matthew's was the earliest written of the four gospels.

____ 2. Jesus teaches that the New Law of Love overthrows the Old Testament Law.

____ 3. The Greek word *Kurios* is best translated as "Lord."

____ 4. The point of the parable of the yeast is the hidden but steady growth of God's kingdom.

____ 5. There are 10 major divisions in Matthew's gospel.

____ 6. Matthew's infancy narrative shows how the Jews will come to accept the universal Messiah.

____ 7. Matthew was written at a time when the early Christians were in confrontation with the Sadducees.

____ 8. The Sermon on the Mount is a classic example of Christian didache.

____ 9. Matthew is the only gospel to use the word for church.

____10. The title Son of Man unites the humanity of Jesus with his function of ushering in God's kingdom.

READING GOD'S WORD

Let's continue the story of the spread of Christianity. Recall that when we last left Paul, he had just returned from Pamphylia and the city of Perga. His first journey took place between 46 and 48.

The second journey took place between 49 and 52. The journey opens with a "violent" quarrel between Paul and Barnabas because of John Mark's desertion of the first mission. They part ways at Antioch with Barnabas and Mark going to Cyprus. Paul recruits Silas and sets out to Syria and Cilicia, encouraging the Christian converts there. Read Paul's adventures on this second journey and trace the journey on the map on page 101. (Use a ----- line to depict this journey.) Then answer the questions below.

Read Acts 15:39-18:22.

16:1-10 Why was Timothy circumcised? ____________________

____________________ What might this say about Paul's attitude to the Jews? ____________________

16:11-15 What leading woman converted to Christianity?

____

16:16-40 Why were Paul and Silas arrested in Philippi?

____________________ Why were they eventually let go? ____________________

17:1-9 What happened in Thessalonika? ____________________

17:10-15: What kind of reception did the disciples get in Beroea?

____

17:16-34: What sin in Athens especially perturbed Paul?

____

What attitude does the author of Acts have towards the Athenians? ____________________

How do the Athenians react to Paul's teaching on the resurrection? ____________________

18:1-11: Why were Aquila and Priscilla in Corinth? ____________________

____

What was Paul's trade? ____________________ Why was Paul so successful in Corinth? ____________________

18:12-17: Gallio, the proconsul of Achaia, refused to prosecute Paul. Why?

____

Summary: Based on what you have read in this section of Acts, write a short paragraph describing Paul's character.

PRAYER REFLECTION

Matthew's gospel contains the greatest of prayers, the Our Father. Let's change it only very slightly and slowly meditate on the petitions.

My Father, who is in heaven,
  holy be your name.
Your kingdom come,
  your will be done on earth as it is in heaven.
Give me this day my daily bread,
  and forgive me my trespasses
  as I forgive those who trespass against me.
And lead me not into temptation,
  but deliver me from evil.
So be it.

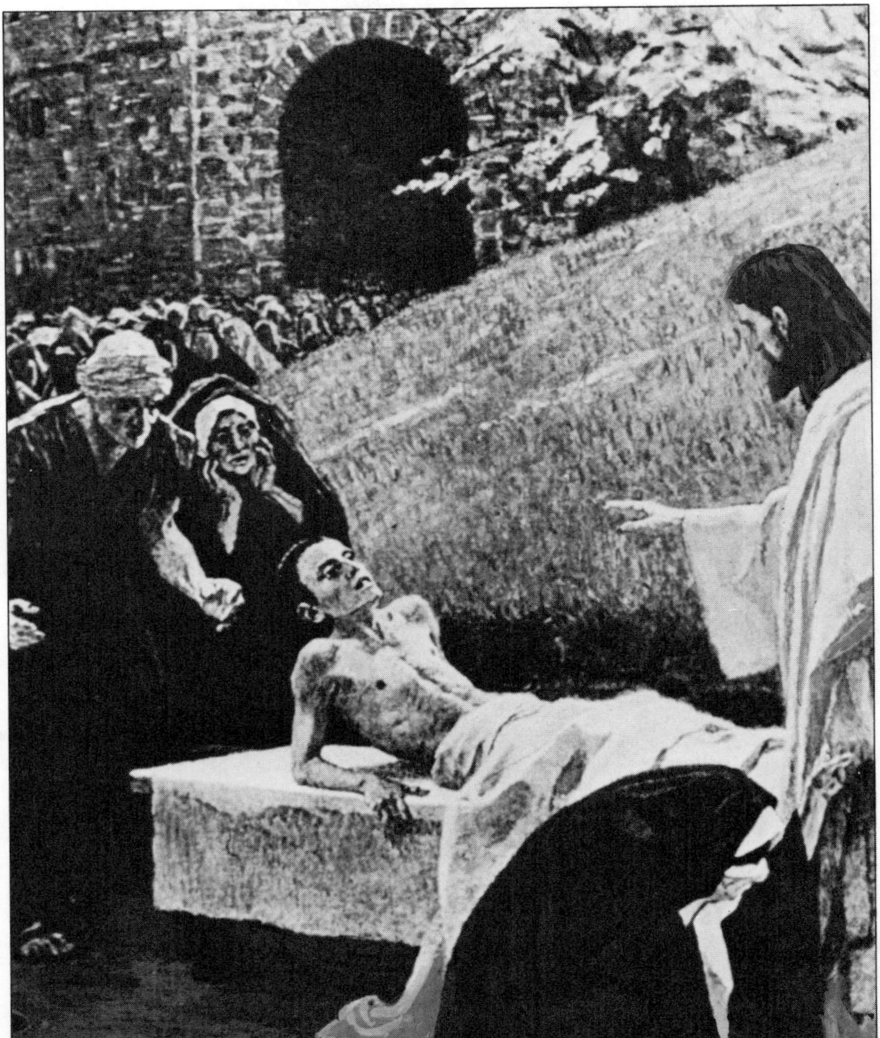

5
Gospel of Luke—Good News for Everyone

> *Seeing that many others have undertaken to draw up accounts of the events that have taken place among us, exactly as these were handed down to us by those who from the outset were eyewitnesses and ministers of the word, I in my turn, after carefully going over the whole story from the beginning, have decided to write an ordered account for you, Theophilus, so that your Excellency may learn how well founded the teaching is that you have received.*
>
> —Luke 1:1-4

The words that you have just read make up the Prologue to Luke's gospel. Many scholars have stated that this Prologue is the best written Greek in the whole New Testament and that Luke is the best writer of any New Testament writer. The French 19th-century thinker Renan even called Luke's gospel "the most beautiful book in the world." Many Christians today agree with that assessment.

The Prologue reveals considerable information about both Luke and his gospel. In these first four verses the author claims that he has carefully researched his material. He states that *many others* have written gospels and that he has carefully gone over this material to write his own version of the good news.

Second, the author addresses his gospel to a certain Theophilus. *Theophilus* is a Gentile-Greek name which means "lover of God."

Significantly, the Acts of the Apostles are also addressed to the same man: "In my earlier work, Theophilus, I dealt with everything Jesus had done and taught . . ." (Acts 1:1). Almost all scholars have concluded, therefore, that the same man was author of both Luke and Acts. Luke-Acts was originally a two-volume work which traced the history of God's people from the time of Israel, through Jesus' story, up to the period of the apostolic church in the Gentile world.

Third, the Prologue states Luke's reason for writing. He wishes to show Theophilus, and all other Gentile "lovers of God," that the instruction they received was well-founded. The overriding concern of Luke's gospel is to offer a defense of Christianity for second-generation Christians. These Christians were living in a world where Christianity was questioned and even opposed. In his gospel and in Acts Luke sought to defend the truth of the good news and to show how Jesus Christ and his Spirit were working in history.

Fourth, Luke writes an ordered account. Of all the gospel writers, Luke has been called the *historian* of the church. He carefully tries to show how God works in human history by linking salvation history to ordinary history. In Luke we see much attention paid to historical detail. For example, note the way he dates the ministry of John the Baptist:

> In the fifteenth year of Tiberius Caesar's reign, when Pontius Pilate was governor of Judaea, Herod tetrarch of Galilee, his brother Philip tetrarch of the lands of Ituraea and Trachonitis, Lysanias tetrarch of Abilene, during the pontificate of Annas and Caiaphas, the word of God came to John son of Zechariah, in the wilderness (Lk 3:1-2).

This history is centered around Jesus' journey to Jerusalem and the apostolic witness about Jesus radiating from that city. As part of this ordered account, Luke highlights the parables of Jesus. These parables fit well into salvation history and have much to tell us about Jesus and the good news of his Father's kingdom.

After the usual introductory exercise, this chapter will treat the following topics:

- authorship, date and outline of Luke
- key themes in Luke's gospel
    - the Spirit in salvation history
    - the gospel of prayer
    - the gospel of joy and peace
    - the gospel for all men and women
- parables in Luke
- the resurrection

TRACING YOUR OWN HISTORY

We have already touched on one of the important themes in Luke's gospel. Luke looks beyond ordinary history to discover how God is working to redeem his people. Salvation history and ordinary history often intersect and can be told together. (For example, you have read how John the Baptist's emergence from the desert intersects with the history of different rulers.) Our own ordinary history also often intersects with how God works in our lives. Examine this truth for yourself.

1. In column one, list some of the high and low points of your life. You might place in parentheses ( ) some key events from world history to help locate your own story.

2. In column two, list some events from your salvation history. These might include your baptism, first communion, confirmation and the like. Also list some events that have had deep personal (even religious) meaning for you, events like the death of a loved one, particular friendships, personal crises and celebrations.

3. Then, wherever you think it is appropriate, draw lines showing where your ordinary history has affected your salvation history. In other words, are there any points where these two connect? Share a few of these connections with a classmate.

   This exercise approximates what Luke did in Luke-Acts.

I. My ordinary history	*II. My salvation history*

AUTHORSHIP, DATE, OUTLINE OF LUKE

The Author

Luke, a Gentile Christian, is mentioned three times by name in the New Testament as a companion of Paul. He also refers to himself when he uses "we" in Acts (16:10-17, 20:5-21:18 and 27:1-28:16). All of these passages underscore the fact that Luke travelled with Paul.

The Greek of Luke's gospel is polished. An ancient tradition says that Luke was an artist and that he even painted a portrait of Mary. Whether he was in fact a painter or not, most scholars would agree that Luke's is the most artistic gospel stylistically.

READING ABOUT LUKE

The three references to Luke in the epistles are Colossians 4:14, Philemon 1:24, 2 Timothy 4:11. Please read them and answer the following two questions:

1. What profession did Luke practice?
2. Based on these references, what kind of relationship did Luke have with Paul?

The Date

Like all the gospels, Luke cannot be dated with any precision. Most commentators suggest anywhere from 70 to 85 or so. This seems probable for the following reasons: 1) Luke used about 65% of Mark's gospel. Thus, Luke had to be written after Mark. 2) Luke's gospel probably refers to the destruction of Jerusalem in A.D. 70 (see 19:43-44 and 21:20). 3) Luke's gospel was widely used by the end of the first century. A common opinion is that Luke wrote his gospel for a Gentile-Christian audience probably in southern Greece (Achaia). He seems to avoid matters with which Gentiles might not be familiar. For example, he eliminates passages about the traditions of the Jews (Mk 7:1-23), the return of the prophet Elijah (Mk 9:11-13) and the references to the Old Law in the Sermon on the Mount. In addition, Luke omits all exclusively Jewish names; for example, he writes "master" (teacher) for rabbi and "lawyer" for scribe. Finally, he calls special attention to Gentiles throughout his gospel; for example, the parable of the Good Samaritan and Jesus' cure of the 10 lepers.

Outline of Luke's Gospel

When Luke wrote, he drew from three major sources: Mark's gospel, *Q* and material known to him (designated "L"). His overriding organizing theme is Jesus' journey to Jerusalem. Everything begins (Zechariah in the Temple in Luke 1:10) and ends (Christians praising God in the Temple in Luke 24:53) in the Holy City. The events of the first two chapters take place in and around Jerusalem; Jesus' third temptation is set there (Lk 4:9-12). In chapter 5 the Pharisees and lawyers come from Jerusalem. In chapter 9 we find a pivotal verse:

> Now as the time drew near for him to be taken to heaven, he resolutely took the road for Jerusalem . . . (v. 51).

With heart and mind set on his destiny in Jerusalem Jesus journeys there to do his Father's will: passion, death, resurrection, glorification. Acts continues this journey theme as the apostles go to the farthest reaches of the Roman Empire to spread the good news about Jesus.

Here is a commonly accepted outline of Luke's gospel:

Prologue: 1:1-4

Part I: From the Temple to the End of the Ministry in Galilee. 1:5-9:50

A. Infancy narratives. 1:5-2:52

B. Preparation for the ministry. 3:1-4:13

C. The ministry in Galilee. 4:14-9:50

Part II: Journey From Galilee to Jerusalem. 9:51-19:27

Part III: Events in Jerusalem. 19:28-24:53

A. Jerusalem ministry. 19:28-21:38

B. The passion. 22-23

C. After the resurrection. 24

KEY READING EXERCISE

By now you have already read many sections of Luke. For example, in chapter 4 you read the infancy narratives. In this exercise you and your classmates will read the middle sections of Luke's gospel, the chapters about Jesus' ministry in Galilee and his journey to Jerusalem. Divide into five groups, each group taking one of the following sections of Luke's gospel:

Group 1: 4:14-6:49 *Group 4:* 13:1-16:31
Group 2: 7:1-9:50 *Group 5:* 17:1-19:27
Group 3: 9:51-12:59

To focus your reading, try to discover concrete examples to illustrate Jesus' attitude to the following groups. Report what you find to your classmates.

1. the poor
2. Gentiles
3. Samaritans
4. women
5. sinners and outcasts

THEMES IN LUKE'S GOSPEL

The Holy Spirit working in salvation history (Read Lk 4:14-30)

In both the gospel of Luke and Acts, the Holy Spirit is portrayed as actively working in human history. What had been promised to Israel in former times has reached its fulfillment in the words, deeds, life, death and resurrection of Jesus Christ. We live in a new age, an age when the Spirit lives with and guides our Lord's church through history until the end of time. Luke's idea of history can be diagrammed this way:

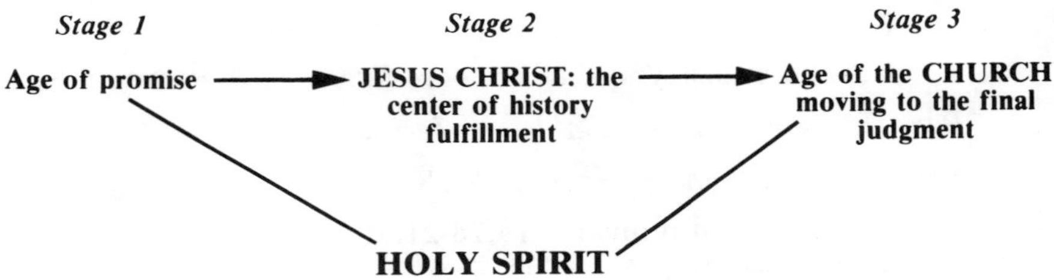

Luke often explicitly refers to the work of the Holy Spirit in both his gospel and Acts. For example, the Spirit is with John the Baptist and his parents. Jesus is conceived by the power of the Spirit. "Filled with the Holy Spirit," Jesus is led into the desert. At the beginning of Jesus' ministry in Galilee, he goes to the synagogue in Nazareth to pray. There he picks up the scroll and reads from the prophet Isaiah:

> *The spirit of the Lord has been given to me,*
> *for he has anointed me.*
> *He has sent me to bring the good news to the poor,*
> *to proclaim liberty to captives*
> *and to the blind new sight,*
> *to set the downtrodden free,*
> *to proclaim the Lord's year of favor* (Lk 4:18-19).

Acts highlights the theme of the Holy Spirit. You have already read in one of the kerygmatic sermons how Peter announced the gift of the Holy Spirit (Acts 2:38-39). Because of the Holy Spirit the gospel spreads steadily. It first reaches the Jews in Jerusalem (Acts 1-7) and then moves on to Judaea, Galilee and Samaria (Acts 8-12). Guided by the Spirit, Paul is instrumental in helping the gospel move from Syria to Greece (Acts 13-19). Then, in Paul's final journey, he goes from captivity in Jerusalem and Caesarea to Rome, taking the good news of Jesus with him to the center of the Empire. Acts concludes on a note of the Spirit's triumph: "Understand, then, that this salvation of God has been sent to the pagans; they will listen to it" (Acts 28:28).

The Gospel of Prayer

For Luke there is a close relationship between the action of the Holy Spirit and prayer. All the synoptic gospels highlight Jesus' prayer. For example, Jesus prayed in Gethsemane after the first multiplication of the loaves and in Capernaum after many cures.

But Luke adds many other examples of Jesus praying. Jesus prayed at his baptism (3:21) and in the desert (5:16). Before he chose his disciples, he prayed a whole night (6:12). Before Peter proclaimed him the Christ, Jesus prayed (9:18); later, he told Peter that he especially prayed for him. He prayed at his transfiguration and taught his disciples how to pray the Our Father. He prayed for those who put him to death while he hung on the cross.

In addition, Luke's Jesus often admonishes his disciples to pray. Two parables teach the lesson of constant prayer, the parable about the friend who came at midnight and the parable about the widow before an unjust judge. The disciples must pray to obtain the gift of the Holy Spirit (11:13); indeed, they must pray at all times (21:36).

The theme of our prayer must be like Jesus' in the garden. Foreseeing his suffering and death Jesus—like any normal person—did not want to undergo the test. But he prayed that his Father's will be done. This is the very prayer we say every time when we recite the Lord's Prayer: "Thy will be done."

LUKE ON MONEY AND WEALTH

A. *If you won some money.* Suppose you won $10,000 in a raffle. List three or four specific things you would do with the money.

____

____

Reflection:

1. What do your choices say about what you value?
2. Did you include other people when you considered your choices? Why or why not?
3. Were your choices geared more toward present happiness or toward your future?
4. Here are statements which some people today believe about money and personal wealth. What do you think about them? Mark your choices according to the following: SA (strongly agree), A (agree), D (disagree), SD (strongly disagree), DK (don't know).

____ a. You can't be both rich and honest.

____ b. The best things in life are not free; they cost money.

____ c. Poverty is the worst of evils.

____ d. Hard work is its own reward.

____ e. Happiness is having enough but not necessarily too much.

____ f. When it comes to money, make a lot.

Discuss each of these with your classmates.

B. Luke's gospel is one of joy and good news for all kinds of people, especially the poor and outcast. Of all the gospels, however, it has some of the most challenging things to say about money. Please read the following passages. Give a brief summary of each. Then discuss the questions which follow.

READING	SUMMARY
Lk 12:13-21—Rich fool	________________
	________________
	________________
Lk 12:33-53—On almsgiving and watchful servants	________________
	________________
	________________
Lk 16:9-13—Right use of money	________________
	________________
	________________

Lk 16:19-31—Rich man and Lazarus ______________________________

____

____

Lk 18:18-30—The rich man ______________________________

____

____

Lk 19:1-10—Zacchaeus ______________________________

____

____

Questions for Discussion

1. In Luke's gospel does Jesus ask everyone to give up his or her money? Why or why not?

2. In your own words what does Jesus seem to be saying about money? Do you agree with it?

3. Why do most people have trouble with these sayings? What do we think money can do for us?

4. In the first parable why is the man called a fool? In the story of Lazarus what saying in Matthew does the rich man ignore? (Check Mt 25:40.)

The Gospel of Joy and Peace

Luke's gospel is filled with a spirit of joy and peace which comes with the good news of Jesus Christ. For example, the announcement by the angel brings great joy to Mary. Her prayerful response, the Magnificat, is a hymn of joy. The birth of the Messiah brings great joy to the angels who announce it and to the people (2:10, 13ff.). In Jesus' ministry, the crowds rejoice over his mighty works. His disciples return from their mission rejoicing. Zacchaeus receives Jesus joyfully. The apostles enter Jerusalem the first time rejoicing and return to the Temple after the ascension with great joy (24:52). The best examples of the spirit of joy in Luke's gospel are the three Lost parables in Luke 15 and the gladness which takes place over the return of sinners.

Connected to joy is the peace of the Lord (7:50 and 8:48), the peace that comes into the world at Jesus' birth. Jesus' great gift is peace, the peace he gives to his followers after his resurrection (Lk 24:36), the peace which Paul shared with the various Christian communities he visited and wrote to. (See the introductions to all Paul's letters.)

Good News for All

The best way to characterize Luke's gospel is to say that it is the universal gospel. More than any other gospel, Luke presents Jesus as the friend of the friendless. Here are four categories of people which Jesus touched in a special way during his ministry.

a. *The poor and lowly.* In Luke, Jesus' identification with the poor is evident from the first. He was born in a manger; poor shepherds visited him first; his mother gave turtledoves, the offering of the poor, at his presentation in the Temple. Describing his own work Jesus said that he came to preach to the poor (7:22). Note Luke's version of the Beatitudes. They are much more pointed and down-to-earth than Matthew's. The first Beatitude reads:

> "How happy are you who are poor: yours is the kingdom of God" (Lk 6:20; refer also to Mt 5:3).

To this Luke adds:

> "But alas for you who are rich: you are having your consolation now" (Lk 6:24).

Jesus identified with the poor and joyfully shared his good news of salvation with them.

b. *Sinners* (Read Lk 7:36-50). Luke mentions that tax collectors and sinners sought out Jesus (5:29-30 and 15:2). He is the only evangelist to record the story of divine forgiveness, the Prodigal Son. He includes Jesus' promise of salvation to the condemned criminal who hung next to him.

One of the most touching stories is that of the notorious woman sinner who rushed into Simon the Pharisee's house and wet Jesus' feet with her tears of repentance. Jesus did not condemn her as

Simon wished him to do. He forgave her and exhorted Simon to love as the woman loved. Jesus came precisely to associate with sinners like this woman. He declared:

> "It is not those who are well who need the doctor, but the sick. I have come not to call the virtuous, but sinners to repentance" (Lk 5:31-32).

c. *Gentiles and Samaritans* (Read Lk 17:11-19 and 10:29-37). Time and again, Luke has good things to say about the Gentiles. For example, he records Jesus telling his townspeople of the faith of two Gentiles from Old Testament times, the widow at Zarephath and Naaman the Syrian (Lk 4:24-27). He also cites the great faith of the centurion, a Gentile, whose servant Jesus cured as a result of that faith (Lk 7:1-10).

The Samaritans, despised by the Jews, also receive much favorable treatment from Jesus. For example, only one leper, a Samaritan, returned to thank Jesus for his cure. He represents a supreme example of faith and gratitude.

For another example, consider the parable of the Good Samaritan. Only Luke gives us this tremendous story, one of the most famous in the world. In this parable Jesus instructed his opponents that love of God must include everyone. Jesus taught the revolutionary insight that one's neighbor extended even to one's enemies. He taught this lesson in a story which would have appeared absurd to his audience. "How can there be a 'good' Samaritan? Is that not a contradiction of terms? There is no such person!" Jesus not only taught a lesson of love through this story but he was also trying to break through the prejudice of people to show them that in God's eyes all people are good, even one's supposed enemies.

d. *Women* (Read Lk 15:8-10). Luke's is also the gospel of women. In our Lord's day, a woman was considered a thing with no right to an education, no legal rights and with no part to play in public life. Luke lovingly portrays women. Note the positive impression you receive of Elizabeth, Mary and Anna—the prophetess—when you read the infancy narrative of Luke. Luke mentions many other women besides: the widow of Nain, the repentant woman in Simon's house, Mary Magdalene, Susanna, Joanna, Martha and Mary (close friends of Jesus), the weeping women of Jerusalem. Finally, Jesus includes women in the parables of the Lost Coin and the Unjust Judge (Lk 18:1-8). The parable of the Lost Coin is especially instructive. There God is compared to a woman who rejoices when she finds a coin. It was simply unheard of for any teacher of Jesus' day to compare God to a woman! By so doing, Jesus broke down people's expectations about their God and, along the way, forced them to reexamine their attitudes toward women.

Summary. Luke's Jesus associates with all kinds of people: the humble, the outcast, sinners, the poor, the despised. This very association is part of the good news of salvation. In and through Jesus the Father's incredible love extends to everyone, but especially to those most in need of it. This is tremendous good news and a reason why Luke's gospel is a joyful one. This is the gospel of salvation.

EXERCISES

A. *God loves all people.* If ever there was a gospel which tried to break through prejudicial thinking, it is Luke's. Jesus tried to show that all people are loved by God and are worthy of our love. He taught that there can be a good Samaritan, that tax collectors are worthy of respect, that Gentiles are also God's people, that women have the same dignity as men.

Prejudice is a serious problem today. Here are some statements describing certain fictional people. Only incomplete information is provided but enough for you to decide what kind of prejudice many people would have about them. Decide how you think most people would judge the character of the person described by encircling the appropriate letter on the continuums given below.

1. Tom is 20 years old and a junior in college. He is 5′3″ tall and has red hair. He makes average grades and dates many different girls.

He probably is

Intelligent	A	B	C	D	E	Stupid
Easygoing	A	B	C	D	E	Hot-tempered
Good-looking	A	B	C	D	E	Ugly

2. Jorge Gonzalez is 36 years old and is employed at a gas station. He is married and has eight kids. He probably is

Friendly	A	B	C	D	E	Unfriendly
Ambitious	A	B	C	D	E	Lazy
Book reader	A	B	C	D	E	Doesn't read books
Reliable	A	B	C	D	E	Unreliable

3. Belinda Smith is 28, black and married to a high school dropout. She works at a restaurant. She probably is

Friendly	A	B	C	D	E	Unfriendly
Intelligent	A	B	C	D	E	Stupid
Outgoing	A	B	C	D	E	Serious
Honest	A	B	C	D	E	Dishonest

4. Mary has a prominent position in a law firm. She is married and has one child. She probably is

Assertive	A	B	C	D	E	Passive
Contented	A	B	C	D	E	Discontented
Rational	A	B	C	D	E	Emotional

5. David is a 16-year-old student in a Catholic high school. He enjoys opera and ballet and works in the summer at a theater for the deaf. He doesn't like sports. He probably is

Popular	A	B	C	D	E	Unpopular
Artistic	A	B	C	D	E	Scientific
Intelligent	A	B	C	D	E	Stupid
Polite	A	B	C	D	E	Rude

For Discussion:

1. Share the reasons you marked the scales as you did.
2. Discuss the prejudices some people might have about these persons.
3. Why are people prejudiced? Can anything be done about this problem? What can you do about your own prejudices?
4. What are some other prejudices people have today against different groups in our society?
5. Based on your reading of the gospels thus far, what prejudices did people have against Jesus?

B. *Mary in the gospels.* Luke lovingly portrays Mary, our Lord's mother and mother to us all. Read what he and other gospel writers say about her. Then, write a 200-word essay entitled, "A Gospel Portrait of Mary."

Lk 1:26-56; 2:1-19, 41-52	Mt 1:18-25
Jn 2:1-12; 19:25-27	Acts 1:14

JESUS' PARABLES

By this time in your study of the New Testament you have read a number of Jesus' parables. Since Luke's gospel contains the most beloved of these stories, we will treat the topic of parables here.

The importance of the parables

The New Testament contains no fewer than 41 parables told by Jesus. The great German scripture scholar Joachim Jeremias says of them: "We find nothing to be compared with the parables of Jesus, whether in the entire intertestamental literature of Judaism, the Essene writings, in Paul, or in Rabbinic literature."

The parables are important for three major reasons: 1) They contain the heart of Jesus' teaching. To know their message is to know much about what Jesus preached. 2) They show Jesus to be an outstanding teacher. Known in his day as a teacher (rabbi), we can today get a flavor of the master storyteller by reflecting on his wonderful word-pictures. 3) They give us a glimpse of how Jesus defended his good news against his opponents. A characteristic of most of the parables is that Jesus told them to defend his message against those who attacked it. The parables not only proclaim the goodness of God but invite those who resist him to accept the good news in faith.

What a parable is

A parable is a story drawn from ordinary life which makes a comparison. A fact from ordinary life or an imagined situation is compared to a religious truth or a spiritual relationship. The ordinary situations ranged from fishing and farming to wedding celebrations and happy meals. They could be about planting seeds, baking bread or winemaking. They sometimes dealt with unjust judges, lost coins and sheep, found treasures, withered trees and mustard seeds, trustworthy servants or wayward sons and a loving father.

A parable was usually first told to make one important point, to teach one significant lesson. The point of comparison always dealt with the nature of God's kingdom. The parable of the Sower is a good example (see Lk 8:4-8 or one of its synoptic parallels, Mk 4:3-8 or Mt 13:3-8). The original punch line of the Sower is that despite the obstacles encountered by the seed, it produced great abundance. The emphasis in this parable, like most, is at the end. Jesus uses this story to assure the crowd that despite meager appearances, the kingdom of God will triumph—and far beyond anyone's expectations. From the small beginnings of Jesus' establishment of the kingdom, God will see to it that the kingdom grows and flourishes.

Settings of the parables

The parables have three settings. In the first setting Jesus told his parables, usually as a defense of his message. The church's early preachers retold these parables, often adapting them to the situations in which early Christians found themselves. This was the second setting, the setting of the early church. Finally, the evangelists wrote down the parables, sometimes changing the context to fit their particular theological slant. We can see this third setting clearly in the parable of the Lost Sheep. So that you can read Matthew and Luke's versions together, both are given here:

Matthew 18:3,12-14

The disciples came to Jesus . . . Then he said, "I tell you solemnly, unless you change and become like little children you will never enter the kingdom of heaven. . . .

"Tell me. Suppose a man has a hundred sheep and one of them strays; will he not leave the ninety-nine on the hillside and go in search of the stray? I tell you solemnly, if he finds it, it gives him more joy than do the ninety-nine that did not stray at all. Similarly, it is never the will of your Father in heaven that one of these little ones should be lost."

Luke 15:2-7

The Pharisees and scribes complained. "This man" they said "welcomes sinners and eats with them." So he spoke this parable to them:

"What man among you with a hundred sheep, losing one, would not leave the ninety-nine in the wilderness and go after the missing one till he found it? And when he found it, would he not joyfully take it on his shoulders and then, when he got home, call together his friends and neighbors? 'Rejoice with me,' he would say 'I have found my sheep that was lost.' In the same way, I tell you, there will be more rejoicing in heaven over one repentant sinner than over ninety-nine virtuous men who have no need of repentance."

How do we explain the slight variations in these two versions? One interpretation is that Jesus used this very same parable to illustrate different points to different groups. More likely, though, these variations are an example of how the gospel writers (as the Christian preachers before them) adapted Jesus' parables to situations in their own lives.

Many scholars think Luke preserves best the original context of Jesus' parables. In this case, the parable of the Lost Sheep illustrates Jesus' concern for sinners. Matthew, on the other hand, adapts the parable as a show of concern for the "little ones" of the Christian community.

Luke stresses God's great joy over one sinner's return. Matthew underscores the Christian leader's obligation to be concerned with the needy members of the community. Matthew seems to take Jesus' original parable about the joy over a returned sinner and turns it into an instruction for Christian leaders to be watchful over their flocks. As you read in Chapter 4, concern with church affairs is a major theme in Matthew's gospel.

MORE ON THE PARABLES

A. *Parables and allegory.* Jesus' parables sometimes lend themselves to allegorization. In an allegory each major element of the story corresponds to some other reality. Luke and the other synoptics record the following allegorical interpretation of the parable of the Sower (see Lk 8:11-15, for example).

	seed	=	word of God
____	those on edge of path	=	tempted by devil
____	those on rocky ground	=	faith can't take root; gives up
____	those on thorny ground	=	worries, riches, pleasures choke faith
____	those on rich soil	=	take word to heart and let it grow to great abundance

1. Check (✓) which kind of soil represents your current commitment to Jesus' word.

2. What are the major temptations in your life which keep you from *really* living God's word?

____

____

3. What thorns—especially worries—keep you from getting closer to Jesus Christ? Is worrying a good thing? Why or why not?

____

____

____

4. List some things you can do that will help the word of God grow in you. Name some people who have helped you grow closer to God.

____

____

____

B. *Try your own hand at interpreting a parable of Jesus.* The Wicked Husbandman seems to contain an allegory. Read it in Luke 20:9-18. With your classmates, come up with an interpretation of this parable. To start off, one allegorical clue is given.

Vineyard owner = ____________________

vineyard = Israel

tenants = ____________________

servants = ____________________

son = ____________________

death of son = ____________________

vineyard given to others = ____________________

crushing by stone = ____________________

Discuss:

To whom is the parable addressed?

____

Do you find any significance in this?

C. *The Good Samaritan* (reread Lk 10:25-37). St. Augustine gave the following interpretation of this parable.

Jerusalem	=	heaven
Jericho	=	world
robbers	=	Satan and bad angels
wounded man	=	Adam
priest	=	Torah
levite	=	prophets
Samaritan	=	Jesus
inn	=	church
Samaritan's return	=	Jesus' return

Two Alternatives:

1. Rewrite the parable. Substitute modern elements into the story. Share your new version with your classmates.
2. With several classmates, plan and enact a skit based on the Good Samaritan.

What the parables teach

The parables contain the good news preached by Jesus. Here is a short summary of their message. References to many of the parables are provided.

1. *Salvation is here.* Jesus ushers in the kingdom as spring brings green leaves to the fig tree (Mt 24:32-35). Like a mustard seed, it begins small but will grow (Mk 4:30-32). God makes it grow by his own design (Mk 4:26-29) and eventually it will reach a great harvest (Lk 8:5-8).

2. *God's kingdom is a free gift.* Everyone is called to God's kingdom, even people we might consider unworthy (Lk 14:15-24). The heavenly banquet is for everyone (Mt 22:1-14). God is like the vineyard owner who freely dispenses his gifts, far beyond what one has earned (Mt 20:1-16). For our part, we are servants who can only joyfully and gratefully accept God's love (Lk 17:7-10).

3. *God loves sinners.* The heart of the good news is God's great love for sinners. He's the good shepherd who seeks out the lost sheep (Lk 15:3-7) or the woman who searches frantically for her lost coin (Lk 15:8-10). He is the merciful father who welcomes back the lost son (Lk 15:11-32). His joy over the returned sinner is great. He only asks in return that we forgive others as we have been forgiven (Mt 18:23-35).

4. *The good news demands an urgent response.* This is not a time for indecision. We must be ever watchful for God's return (Lk 12:35-40). The Bridegroom (Jesus) can come at any time (Mt 25:1-10). Some people will refuse to respond, like tenants in a vineyard who refuse to give the owner his proper share (Mt 21:33-46). They will complain like little children who are acting like spoilsports (Lk 7:29-35). But, in the end, they will be destroyed. Wheat will be separated from weeds (Mt 13:24-30), and bad fish will be tossed out of the net (Mt 13:47-50). If the kingdom is found, one must be wily like a crafty businessman in order to gain it (Lk 14:25-35). It is like finding a pearl or a hidden treasure; one must sell all to gain it (Mt 13:44-46).

5. *The good news of God's kingdom demands repentance.* Having accepted the gift of the kingdom, we must be prepared for the feast (Mt 22:1-14). We must be faithful (Mt 21:28-32). We must ask for God's forgiveness, not like Pharisees but like sinful tax collectors (Lk 18:9-14). We must forgive others (Mt 5:25-26) and pray without ceasing, like the friend begging for bread at midnight (Lk 11:5-8) or the woman badgering the unjust judge (Lk 18:1-8). Above all else, we must love everyone, even our enemies, following the example of the Good Samaritan (Lk 10:25-37). Finally, the believer must put the goods of this world into proper perspective; for example, money is a means to heaven, not an end in itself (Lk 12:13-21; 16:1-12).

6. *The kingdom may bring suffering.* Those who suffer for Jesus will have their reward while those who take advantage of others will be punished later (Lk 16:19-31). If we respond

to the "least of these," we respond to Jesus and will be rewarded for our efforts (Mt 25:31-46).

READING SOME PARABLES

Directions: Read each of the following parables and answer the questions below.

A. *The Two Builders* (Lk 6:47-49)

What is the point of this parable?

____

____

B. *Places at Table* (Lk 14:7-11)

1. What is the point of this parable?

____

____

2. What might it mean for us today?

____

____

C. *The Capricious Children* (Lk 7:31-35)

1. Who are "the men of this generation"?

____

____

2. What does Jesus compare them to?

____

____

D. *The Prodigal Son* (Lk 15:11-32)

1. To whom does Jesus address this parable? (Check vv. 1-3.)

____

____

2. This parable has often been referred to as the parable of the Loving Father. Is this an appropriate title? How is the father in the parable like God?

3. Who might the second son represent? What is the father's attitude toward him?

4. What is the theme of the parable?

THE RESURRECTION OF JESUS

Read Luke 24.

Central to Christian belief in Jesus is our belief in his resurrection from the dead. Let us end this chapter by looking at Luke's narrative about this most important event in history.

Purpose of the narratives

All the gospel writers include resurrection stories to end their gospels. These stories announce the incredible good news that Jesus has risen from the dead, that he lives today and that we can still "keep in touch" with him.

The narratives in each of the gospels usually include the following elements: 1) an empty tomb; 2) appearances by Jesus; 3) instructions given by Jesus; 4) an ascension. Concerning the empty tomb it is important to note that it does not cause faith. In Luke's gospel, for example, the apostles think the women's report about the empty tomb is sheer nonsense. When they see for themselves, they are amazed, but nothing is said about belief.

Appearances of Jesus do help the apostles to believe. In Luke's gospel, three appearances are reported: one to the two disciples on the road to Emmaus; one to Peter; and a third to the apostles. The Emmaus story is particularly delightful. The disciples are kept from recognizing Jesus. He explains scripture to them first and then shows himself "in the breaking of the bread." The expression "to break bread" is a clear reference to the Eucharist. One of the main points Luke emphasizes is that the resurrected Jesus lives in the Eucharist. He can be recognized and met when Christians celebrate the Lord at Mass.

The appearances reveal that Jesus is not a ghost. Luke emphasizes this by having the resurrected Jesus eat fish. John does the same kind of thing by having Jesus ask Thomas to touch his wounds (Jn 20:24-29). Jesus is not a ghost; neither is he a corpse that is breathing again. He is alive in a *transformed* body, a glorified body which still has an aspect of "bodiliness" to it.

The instructions Jesus gives in Luke's gospel help the apostles to understand that Jesus fulfills the Old Testament. His instructions get them ready for the descent of the Spirit and their missionary task to preach, from Jerusalem, the good news of God's forgiveness. Matthew reports Jesus' instructions to the apostles to preach the gospel to the end of the world (Mt 28:16-20). John recounts Jesus' commission to the apostles to forgive sin (Jn 20:19-23). The second ending of Mark's gospel has the same kind of commission (Mk 16:15-16).

What exactly happened?

We do not really know. The evangelists were not concerned with putting together any kind of order in the resurrection events. They do not give a simple, coherent, orderly or chronological account of what took place. Rather, they were primarily interested in witnessing to Christian faith. They collected together stories that were remembered by various Christians years after the event. In these stories, they were saying basically two things:

- Jesus is alive and active in the community of believers. We know that he is alive because we have seen him (in 1 Cor 15:3-8 Paul reports that over 500 people saw him) and experience his presence even now; for example, when we break bread in his name.

- Because Jesus rose from the dead, we are all destined for a life of resurrected glory. Paul says this time and again in his letters (see Col 1:17-18, and especially 1 Cor 15:12-34). Jesus' resurrection gives new meaning to our life. It gives us hope that death does not end it all. It promises eternal life in a loving union with the Father.

Prominent scripture scholar Norman Perrin answers the question about what happened this way:

> In some way they (the apostles) were granted a vision of Jesus which convinced them that God had vindicated Jesus out of his death, and that therefore the death of Jesus was by no means the end of the impact of Jesus upon their lives and upon the world in which they lived. Very much to the contrary, since Jesus as risen commis-

sioned them to new tasks and to new responsibilities, they found confidence in themselves and in the future of the world in which they lived precisely because they were responding to Jesus as risen, and because they were now living in a world in which Jesus was risen (*The Resurrection According to Matthew, Mark, Luke* (Philadelphia: Fortress Press, 1977), p. 83).

Meaning for us

Jesus' resurrection is absolutely central to our faith in Jesus. We are a joyous people because our Lord lives and we can contact him today in the Christian community. We celebrate a life that we know will end in death because we know that death will bring an absolutely wonderful new life in the Lord. We try to imitate Jesus by loving others because we know this is the way to eternal life. In faith, we know that sin has been conquered by Jesus because its ultimate effect—death—has been overcome by him. We are a people of hope because suffering and death do not conquer us. This is the good news of Jesus Christ!

FOR REFLECTION AND STUDY

A. *Belief in the resurrection.* Check off those statements which reflect your belief.

____ 1. Jesus is alive.

____ 2. I am destined for eternal life with him.

____ 3. The Lord lives today in the Christian community.

____ 4. I can receive the risen Lord in the Eucharist.

____ 5. I will one day have a resurrected body.

____ 6. Death does not end it all.

____ 7. Death leads to new life.

B. *More on the resurrection.* Read Matthew 28, Mark 16, and John 20-21. Then do the following:

List at least three differences between and among these three accounts of the resurrection:

	Mark	Matthew	John
a.			
b.			
c.			

Discuss:

1. Do you see any significance in Jesus appearing first to Mary Magdalene (Jn 20:11-18)? Explain.
2. If the evangelists wished to fabricate the stories about Jesus' resurrection, would they have allowed different versions of the events to be written? Why or why not? Do these different accounts argue strongly that something marvelous *did* happen?
3. What will the resurrected body be like? (To answer this, read 1 Corinthians 15:12-34.)
4. Can you share with your classmates any event in your life which absolutely convinces *you* that Jesus Christ lives and is alive in your life?
5. Discuss this statement: Without any resurrection there would be no Christianity.

SUMMARY

1. Luke wrote his gospel to Gentile Christians to defend the truth of Christianity and to show the Holy Spirit at work in human history. Luke himself was probably a companion to Paul. His gospel is a literary masterpiece and shows concern for historical detail.

2. Luke wrote his gospel between 70 and 85. Its main outline suggests a journey theme, a theme taken up in Acts. Luke's gospel is known as the gospel of prayer and the gospel of joy and peace.

3. Luke's gospel highlights the good news of Jesus preached especially to the following groups: the poor and lowly, sinners, Gentiles and Samaritans, women.

4. The parables, stories drawn from ordinary life which teach about God's kingdom, are characteristic of Jesus' teaching. They ordinarily teach one point. Their settings include Jesus' ministry, the early church and the written gospels themselves.

5. The parables of Jesus teach that salvation is here and that God's kingdom is a free gift. They teach about God's love for sinners and the necessity to repent and urgently respond to the kingdom. And they tell us that disciples of Jesus may have to suffer.

6. Belief in the resurrection is central to Christian faith. The Emmaus story in Luke's gospel proclaims the truth that Jesus lives and can be met in the Eucharist. The various stories teach two truths: Jesus is alive and active in the world; and we also will rise from the dead and are destined for eternal life with the Lord.

EVALUATION

Directions: Respond to the following questions:

1. To whom are both the gospel of Luke and Acts addressed?

____

2. Both Luke and Acts show the activity of the ______________ in human history.

3. What city is given a prominent position in Luke's gospel?

____

4. Briefly discuss Jesus' attitude to money as presented in Luke.

____

____

5. Give an interpretation of the parable of the Lost Coin.

____

____

6. Which of the following parables teach about God's love for sinners?

   Rich Man and Lazarus   Lost Sheep   Unjust Judge   Sower
   Prodigal Son

7. What is the meaning of the parable of the Good Samaritan?

____

____

8. What does Jesus teach in the parable of the Mustard Seed?

____

____

9. The resurrection means that Jesus returned to the *same* kind of life which he left when he died. (True or False) ____________

10. List three ways that Christians believe Jesus can be met today.

   a. ____________________   b. ____________________

   ____________________   ____________________

   c. ____________________

   ____

READING GOD'S WORD

Paul ended his second missionary journey at Caesarea where he greeted the church there. He began his final journey from Antioch, his headquarters for missionary activity. This final journey took place between 53 and 57.

Read about Paul's adventures on this third journey and trace the journey on the map on page 101. (Use a straight line ________ this time.) Then answer the questions below.

Read Acts 18:22-21:16.

18:24-28: At what was Apollos good? ____________________

19:1-7: What is the difference between the baptism of John and Christian baptism? ____________________

19:11-20: What were the Jewish exorcists unable to do at Ephesus? ____________________ Why not? ____________________

19:23-41: Why was Demetrius upset over Paul? ____________________ What happened? ____________________

____

20:1-6: Who does the "we" refer to in this section? (Read page 137 of the text if you are in doubt.) ____________________

____

20:7-12: What rather amusing incident took place at Troas?

____

20:17-38: In his address to the elders of Ephesus, what did Paul fear most for them after he left? ____________________

21:1-14: Why was Paul warned not to go to Jerusalem? ____________________ How did he respond? ____________________

____

PRAYER REFLECTION

Father, you teach a message of love because you are love.
You give your Son to me.
You give me life, friends, health, food.
You forgive my sins.
You love me with an incredible love—a love I don't have to earn.
You love me as I am and I thank you for that.

In return, you teach that I must love, too.
But it is so hard, at times, to do so.
I get tired and angry and impatient and jealous.

So I ask, help me to love, especially those who are difficult to love: people I don't like
"friends" who abandon me
the old, the sick, those different from me.

Thanks, Lord, for your love.

I shall try to return that love.

Just be patient with me. Amen.

6
Gospel of John—Word Made Flesh

In the beginning was the Word:
the Word was with God
and the Word was God.

The Word was made flesh,
he lived among us,
and we saw his glory,
the glory that is his as the only Son of the Father,
full of grace and truth.

—John 1:1,14

Even from the opening verses of John's gospel you can sense something different about it. The first verse recalls the majesty of the very first line of Genesis: "In the beginning God created the heavens and the earth" (Gn 1:1). None of the other gospels opens with such a majestic line.

As the last gospel written, John represents the summit of New Testament theological reflection on Jesus. St. Jerome remarked that the author of the fourth gospel was "saturated with revelation." From the earliest centuries the author of John's gospel has been given the name, "the theologian."

You might recall that the symbol for John the Evangelist is the eagle. The eagle soars to great heights and dwells in lofty places. It has the keenest vision and reputedly can gaze steadily at the sun. The eagle image was well chosen.

John's gospel represents the early church's most profound attempt to understand the meaning of Jesus. Although the vocabulary is simple, almost every phrase is loaded with powerful meaning which goes beyond the words used. Compared to the other gospels, the content, language, style and portrait of Jesus in John's gospel are unique.

The Prologue to John's gospel is the key to unlocking its profound meaning. This majestic hymn contains most of the major themes of the gospel. Pause here and read the Prologue slowly and meditatively, reflecting on the meaning of the words:

Read John 1:1-18.

The Prologue in brief

A central theme in John's gospel concerns its Christology, that is, its reflection on the meaning of Jesus. John has a "Christology from above" in which we see the following movement: Christ comes to us first from above (1:1-13); he reveals the Father and takes us to him (1:14-18). John's Christology is shown in the following diagram:

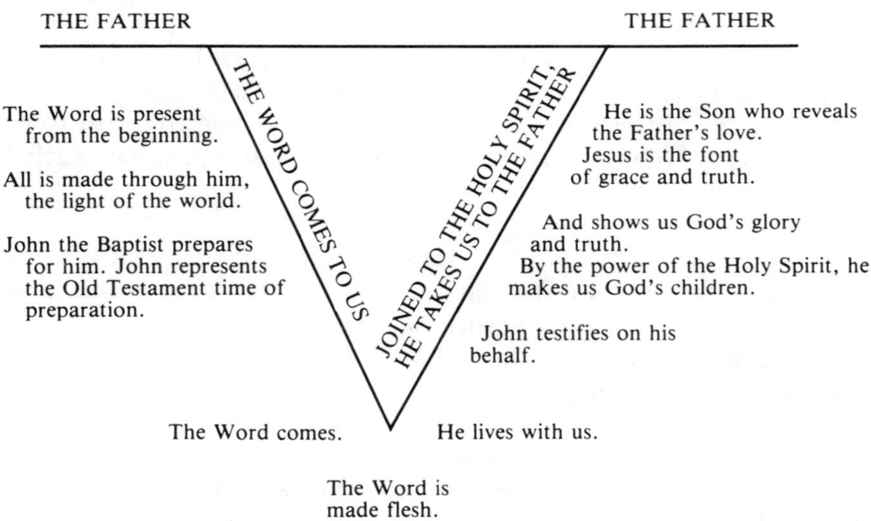

Here then is a list of these major themes all of which are introduced in the Prologue:

- Jesus is God's creative Word who existed from all time. (Mark begins his gospel with Jesus' public life. Matthew traces Jesus' origins back to Abraham. Luke shows Jesus' relationship to Adam. Only John shows how Jesus pre-existed from all time with the Father.)

- Major conflicts are presented:
  —the light of Christ vs. the darkness of the world which will not acknowledge him
  —belief in Jesus which brings life (we become children of God) vs. unbelief
  —truth vs. untruth

- The testimony of John the Baptist is given. He is not the Christ but testifies on Jesus' behalf. (This theme prepares for the testimony of others in the gospel: the Samaritan woman, the crowd at Lazarus' raising, the twelve, the "beloved disciple," the Father, Jesus himself, the Holy Spirit. Jesus' miracles and the scriptures also reveal who Jesus is.)

- Jesus reveals God's glory. It is he who shows the power and radiance and love of God. Through him, God is made present to us. He is God-made-visible. He is God-in-the-flesh.

As you read through John's gospel, try to keep these themes in mind. This chapter will treat the following topics:

- authorship, date and outline of John
- John's gospel and the synoptics
- The Book of Signs
- The Book of Glory

TWO IMAGES IN JOHN'S GOSPEL

A. *Growth.* One of the beautiful images of Jesus in John's gospel is the image of the vine. He is the vine and we are the branches who derive our life from him. He wants us to be alive, growing branches. What keeps us alive is how we love. Let us reflect on this image by doing the following:

1. Read John 15:1-17: The True Vine.
2. Read 1 Corinthians 12:31-13:13 where Paul spells out in more detail what is meant by love.
3. Judge how alive you are by how much you love. Measure your progress on the following growth chart. Mark an "X" on the line to show where you think you are now.

GROWTH CHART

1. How do I judge my patience with others, for example, with my parents?

   I'm very patient ________________________ I'm very impatient

2. How kind am I? Do I go out of my way to help lonely or unpopular classmates?

   I'm very kind ________________________ I'm very unkind

3. How secure am I? Do I need to boast about my achievements?

   I'm very quiet about my achievements ________________________ I brag a lot

4. How do I relate to others? Do I resent them?

   I'm very open to others ________________________ I'm very jealous

5. How is my endurance? Am I willing to accept setbacks?

   I'm open to whatever comes ________________________ I'm a chronic complainer

6. Do I forgive others?

   I'm very forgiving ________________________ I hold grudges

Using the Corinthians passage, make up three more growth assessment statements here. Judge yourself on each.

7. ________________________

   ____

8. ________________________

   ____

9. ______________________________

____

B. *Light and darkness.* You have observed in John's Prologue that light is a major theme in his gospel. The word *light* is used seven times there. Reflect on the light image that appears throughout John's gospel. With your classmates:

1. Make a list of the many positive things that light represents.
2. Make a list of the many negative things that darkness represents.
3. Read the following verses in John's gospel and discuss the questions:

   a. 3:19-21 Are more sins committed at night or during the day?

   ____

   Can you give any examples?

   ____

   ____

   How is light related to truth?

   ____

   ____

   b. 8:12 To what is light compared? How might this be related to birth?

   ____

   ____

   c. 12:35-36 What does Jesus ask from his followers?

   ____

   ____

4. *Discuss:*

   Why did Jesus use the image of light?

____

AUTHORSHIP, DATE, OUTLINE OF JOHN

The Author

No one knows for sure who wrote the fourth gospel. The earliest tradition about its authorship comes from Irenaeus, a church Father who wrote around the year 180. He attributed the gospel to John, the disciple of Jesus, son of Zebedee and brother to James. For a long time this tradition was accepted.

Today, however, scholars note the complex nature of John's gospel. They point to many characteristics in the gospel which indicate that it was written in a number of stages and may even have been produced in several editions. For example, some material is written down twice with wording only slightly changed (see 6:35-50 and 6:51-58). For another example, they point to chapter 21 as an appendix which was added later by someone other than the original author.

There seems to be agreement that the gospel is based ultimately on the witness of the apostle John, son of Zebedee. This same John is probably the beloved disciple mentioned in the fourth gospel. Around him grew a community of followers who took his testimony, reflected on it prayerfully and wrote a gospel which addressed the concerns of their own particular community. This community seemed to be made up of Christians who had come from different backgrounds—many Jews from Palestine, Samaritans and some Gentiles. The community suffered at the hands of the Jews who expelled them from the synagogues after the Roman Revolt. The gospel was put together in its final form by an unknown editor, perhaps a close disciple of John the apostle. Tradition sometimes identifies this final editor as John the Elder who wrote the three letters of John. (He is mentioned by name in 2 John 1:1 and 3 John 1:1.)

READING ABOUT THE BELOVED DISCIPLE

Read in John the following references to the beloved disciple, John, son of Zebedee, and discuss the questions:

13:23 19:26 20:2-10 21:7,20-23,24

1. How was this disciple especially favored by Jesus?

2. Describe him in relation to Peter. Do you see any significance in the beloved disciple stepping aside to allow Peter to enter the tomb first (20:3-5)?
3. What verse do scholars use to reach the conclusion that the beloved disciple had a hand in writing the gospel of John?

The Date

John's gospel was written between 90 and 100, probably from Ephesus in modern-day Turkey. The earliest fragment from any of the New Testament books was found this century in Egypt. This early fragment (known as the John Rylands Greek papyrus) is a selection from John's gospel and has been dated at around 130. What this discovery shows is that the fourth gospel was certainly used far and wide in the Roman Empire only 30 or 40 years after its composition.

The very end of John's gospel gives us the reason why it was written:

> There were many other signs that Jesus worked and the disciples saw, but they are not recorded in this book. These are recorded so that you may believe that Jesus is the Christ, the Son of God, and that believing this you may have life through his name (Jn 20:30-31).

This short statement of purpose shows that the evangelist was not interested in recounting all that Jesus did; he was not interested in simply giving the same kind of information that could be found in the synoptic gospels. His prime aim was to help his audience believe that Jesus is God's Son. The focus in the fourth gospel is clearly on Jesus. We might say that this gospel *interprets* the many traditions about Jesus, the familiar stories that people knew. This interpretation attempts to show how Jesus is the fullness of God's revelation, how he alone is savior of the world.

The second part of the quote is important, too. John's gospel attempts to lead the reader to *belief* because belief brings eternal life. The theme of eternal life is important in John's gospel. The concept of "eternal life" is similar to the idea of "kingdom of God" in the synoptic gospels. In John, eternal life is something we can have right now—not only in some distant future—if only we believe in Jesus Christ, the Son of God.

Outline of John's Gospel

What did the author of John's gospel use when he wrote his gospel? What were his sources? There seem to be three that are agreed upon. First, the fourth gospel reinterprets many of the traditions about Jesus. The author is very familiar with much that went into the synoptic gospels. Some scholars even maintain that he might have directly known Mark's gospel. A common example used to back up this conclusion is the arrangement of chapter 6 in John which seems to rely directly on Mark.

Second, John seems to have had access to a separate tradition of the miracles of Jesus called the signs source. Some of the seven signs treated in John's gospel appear in the synoptics as well, for example, the multiplication of loaves. But others are unique to John, such as the wine miracle at Cana and the raising of Lazarus. As we shall see later in this chapter, John attaches special meaning to the signs of Jesus.

Third, John used the passion narrative which had been formulated before any of the gospels were written.

Characteristic of John's gospel are the long discourses of Jesus which include a special kind of language using opposites: truth and falsehood, light and darkness, above and below. This language is known as *dualism*—two extremes are contrasted. You have already seen another characteristic of the fourth gospel in the last section of this chapter: a Christology where the Word descends from above only to reascend to the Father. These characteristics led some people to think that John was deeply influenced by the gnostic philosophy which was prominent in the second century, a philosophy which used dualistic concepts. (Gnosticism was an antiworldly religious movement which was considered heretical by the church.)

However, the discovery of the Dead Sea scrolls (Essene literature) has shown that this kind of language was also common to the Jews. Few people today believe that John was greatly influenced by gnosticism. In fact he rejected their beliefs by showing both in his gospel and in his three letters that Jesus was God-become-flesh. By emphasizing the bodily aspect of Jesus, John rejected a key belief of the gnostics who held that the body was evil.

The simplest outline of John's gospel looks like this:

Prologue	1:1-18
Part I: Book of Signs	1:19-12:50
Part II: Book of Glory	13:1-20:31
Epilogue	21:1-25

KEY READING EXERCISES

A. *For everyone.* Read John's second letter which consists of 13 verses. Then, in light of what you have just read, discuss the significance of verses 7-11.

B. *Book of Signs.* Below you will find a more detailed outline of the first part of John's gospel. This outline follows the Jesus story from the opening week of his ministry up through various religious feasts to the Last Supper. Divide the readings among five groups. Each group is responsible for answering the lead questions asked here. Share the results of your research with the rest of the class. Each person should end up with a completed outline of the Book of Signs.

I. *The Opening Week or So* (1:19-2:11)
   - A. What did John the Baptist say?
   - B. What happened next?
   - C. What role did Mary play at the wedding feast at Cana?

II. *From Cana to Cana* (2-4)
   - A. Why did Jesus cleanse the Temple?
   - B. Summarize the dialogue with Nicodemus.
   - C. Summarize the dialogue with the Samaritan Woman.
   - D. What was the second sign at Cana?

III. *Jesus and the Jewish Feasts* (5-10)
   - A. 5:1-47 *The Sabbath:* What happened and what was said?
   - B. 6:1-71 *Passover:* What happened and what was said?
   - C. 7:1-8:59 *Tabernacles:* List three key teachings of Jesus.
   - D. 9:1-10:21 *Between Feasts*
     1. Discuss the meaning of the cure of the blind man.
     2. What famous image does Jesus teach?
   - E. 10:22-42 *Dedication:* What claim is made?

IV. *Jesus Nears the Hour of Glory* (11-12)
   - A. Chapter 11: What happened and what was said?
   - B. Chapter 12: What happened? List two teachings of Jesus.

JOHN AND THE SYNOPTICS COMPARED

When John's gospel is compared with the synoptic gospels a number of interesting observations emerge. A striking point is that in John's gospel Jesus celebrates at least three Passover feasts during his public ministry: after the wine miracle at Cana (Jn 2:13), at the multiplication of loaves (Jn 6:4), and a final one during Passion Week (Jn 11:55). The synoptics record only one such celebration by Jesus. Reading the synoptics, therefore, you get the idea that Jesus' public ministry lasted only one year; reading John, you conclude that his ministry had to last more than two years.

Here are some other comparisons between John and the synoptics:

Only in John	*Only in synoptics*
wedding at Cana (2:1-11)	birth narratives
story of Nicodemus (3:1-21)	baptism of Jesus
dialogue with Samaritan woman (4:1-42)	temptation in the desert
healing at pool of Bethzatha (5:1-9)	transfiguration
raising of Lazarus (11:1-44)	agony in Gethsemane
washing of apostles' feet (13:1-20)	Last Supper in upper room
	parables
	exorcisms

Besides these differences in content, John uses different literary techniques. He presents, for example, Jesus' teachings in the form of long, well-developed theological discourses. The synoptics, on the other hand, either group the different sayings of Jesus into a series (like the parables in Luke 15) or into groups of related sayings (like Matthew's Sermon on the Mount). John's pattern of narration starts with

an event that moves to

a dialogue between Jesus and the other characters that ends in

a *monologue* in which Jesus gives a theological teaching.

See how this pattern emerges in the following exercise.

Discourse with Nicodemus. Read John 2:23-3:21. Then answer these questions.

1. What *event*(s) triggered the discussion with Nicodemus?

____

____

2. What was the theme of the *dialogue* between Jesus and Nicodemus?

____

____

3. What is the point of Jesus' *monologue* which begins in 3:11?

____

____

____

THE BOOK OF SIGNS

By now you have read about a number of Jesus' miracles. A word about miracles is in order here. First we'll look at the general meaning behind all of Jesus' miracles. Then we'll briefly discuss how John's gospel understood the miracles of Jesus. Finally each of John's miracles will be listed with a short explanation. Somewhat more attention will be given to the raising of Lazarus because it contains many of the themes of John's gospel.

The Meaning of Jesus' Miracles

1. *As signs of God's power, miracles show that God's kingdom is breaking into human history.* Jesus saw himself as the bringer of God's good news. When the imprisoned John the Baptist asks about Jesus' identity, Jesus answers by pointing to the deeds he performs: the blind see, the lame walk, lepers are cured, the deaf hear, the dead are raised to life, the poor have good news preached to them. Salvation is taking place! The awaited time has come. God's kingdom

brings wholeness and new life. The healing miracles especially point to this tremendous reality.

2. *The miracles indicate who Jesus is.* After Jesus walked on water, the occupants of the boat said, "Truly, you are the Son of God" (Mt 14:33). Jesus is the one who casts out demons. He has power over Satan. He must be the one who acts for God and ushers in the kingdom. He heals on the Sabbath because he is Lord of the Sabbath. In short, the miracles tell us who Jesus is.

3. *Faith is associated with miracles as signs.* Sometimes faith is necessary for a miracle. We saw this in Mark's gospel where Jesus could work no miracles in his hometown of Nazareth except for some healings because of the lack of faith there (Mk 6:5). Jesus refused to perform miracles for show. Faith in him was necessary. After several healings Jesus praised people for their faith and said that their faith helped them.

Sometimes a miracle came first and led to faith. We saw this in Matthew's version of Jesus walking on the sea. The person had to be open and receptive to Jesus if faith were to grow. The gospels also report how Jesus' miracles brought severe opposition. For example, although some Jews believed in Jesus after he brought Lazarus back to life, others did not and immediately plotted to kill Jesus (Jn 11:45-54).

John's Concept of Miracle

The synoptics use the Greek word *dynamis* for miracle. It means "an act of power." Their primary concern is to show how Jesus establishes God's kingdom by overthrowing the power of Satan. The miracles were Jesus' chief weapon in the war against Satan. By casting out demons, curing sickness, raising the dead and calming the forces of nature, the synoptics show Jesus powerfully bringing God's salvation.

John's main concern in reporting the miracles is somewhat different. John alone refers to miracles as *signs (semeia* in the Greek). He does not wish to show Jesus as some magician or wonderworker. Miracles are events that *reveal* God. It takes faith to comprehend their deeper meaning. The long discourses in John's gospel help the believer understand the *sign*ificance of the miracles/signs of Jesus.

The Seven Signs in John

The first part of John's gospel highlights seven signs/miracles of Jesus.

Sign 1: Water into wine at Cana (Jn 2:1-12). Before his public ministry, Jesus changed water into wine. There are a number of ways to interpret this miracle. We see, for example, that Mary can intercede for us; that through Jesus we are transformed into new life as water was changed into wine; that the water symbolizes baptism which purifies us; that the wine points to the Eucharist which brings spiritual life.

Sign 2: Cure of the nobleman's son (Jn 4:46-54). The dying son is cured through Jesus' word. The faith of the father, a court official from Capernaum, prompted Jesus to act on the son's behalf. The meaning of this sign may be stated this way: Faith in Jesus coupled with his life-giving word can rescue us from spiritual death.

Sign 3: Cure of the paralytic at the pool of Bethzatha (Jn 5:1-47). A sick man, lame for 38 years, is cured by Jesus on the Sabbath. The meaning: The Father makes Jesus the source of life. Our response must be faith in him so that we have eternal life.

Sign 4: Feeding of the five thousand (Jn 6:1-14). Jesus feeds the hungry crowd which has followed him. The people wish to make him king, but Jesus flees their misguided enthusiasm. Later, at the synagogue in Capernaum, Jesus interprets the miracle: He is the bread of life who gives himself for the world. We are to partake of this bread to gain eternal life. This sign clearly foreshadows the Eucharist.

Sign 5: Jesus walks on water (Jn 6:16-21). The meaning of this miracle is hidden in the words "It is I. Do not be afraid" (Jn 6:21). *It is I (ego eimi* in Greek) is the Jewish name for God (another translation is "I am," Yahweh). The meaning: God is present in Jesus because Jesus is God! We who are the disciples of the Lord need not fear because Jesus is with us. Through the centuries the church has sometimes been pictured as a boat adrift on stormy seas. Because of Jesus the church need never fear; he is always with us.

Sign 6: Cure of the blind man (Jn 9:1-41). After washing in the pool of Siloam, a man born blind is cured by Jesus. The meaning: We are all like the blind man. From birth we are spiritually blind and unable to see through the darkness. Only the light can help us to see. Faith in Jesus enables us to see the light and overcome our spiritual blindness.

Please read John 11:1-44.

Sign 7: The raising of Lazarus (Jn 11:1-44). Many of the themes of John's gospel appear in this sign. The narrative of the miracle takes place in three scenes.

> **Scene 1** Jesus is on the other side of the Jordan with his apostles. He receives news that his friend Lazarus is sick and near death. Jesus does not go to him immediately. He says that Lazarus' sickness will not end in death but that through it both the Father and Son will be glorified (Jn 11:14). The apostles do not wish Jesus to go for fear of his life. Jesus refers again to the light and the need to walk in the light. Knowing that Lazarus already has died, Jesus assures his apostles that Lazarus will awaken from his rest (Jn 11:11). The apostles misunderstand Jesus, thinking he is talking about sleep. Jesus explains to the apostles exactly what he means. Finally, Jesus instructs the disciples that what will take place will help them believe.
>
> In this one short scene John has touched on many themes which appear regularly in his gospel. Jesus has come to glorify the Father. He is light of the world which leads believers out of darkness. Jesus' words are subject to misunderstanding which needs clarification. The sign Jesus performs will help belief.

Scene 2 Jesus and his disciples go to Bethany, only two miles from Jerusalem. Many Jews are there to sympathize with Mary and Martha. Martha displays openness to Jesus when she says: "But I know that, even now, whatever you ask of God, he will grant you" (Jn 11:22). When Jesus assures Martha that Lazarus will rise again, Martha can only think of the general resurrection from the dead at the end of time. But Jesus intends something more when he says these important words:

"I am the resurrection.
If anyone believes in me, even though he dies he will live
and whoever lives and believes in me
will never die" (Jn 11:25-26).

In this one important quote the themes of resurrection, belief, life and eternal life are pulled together. The "I am" leaves the reader with little doubt that Jesus is the Lord.

Scene 3 The scene shifts to the tomb of Lazarus. Mary, Lazarus' sister, chastises Jesus for not preventing Lazarus' death. Little does she know what is to take place. Jesus weeps for his friend Lazarus and perhaps also because people lack faith. Despite Martha's reminder that the body is decomposing in the tomb, Jesus requests that the stone be rolled away. Jesus thanks the Father for having heard his prayer. His prayer should make it easier for the bystanders to recognize that what is going to happen is God's action. Jesus calls for Lazarus to emerge. He does! Jesus gives one last instruction for Lazarus to be unbound from his burial cloth so that he can go free.

In this, the most dramatic of all miracles, Jesus reveals himself as the giver of life. Faith in him leads to life. This last miracle of Jesus points to his own resurrection and glorification. Just as Jesus has broken death's power when he raises Lazarus, so his own death leads to life. Through his death he will give eternal life to the faithful.

This last sign of Jesus stands as a summary of all the signs and many of the theological themes in John's gospel. Jesus is the way to life. He is the resurrection. He is light. He is God (I AM). We must believe in him to have what he has accomplished for us: eternal life in union with the Father, Son and Holy Spirit.

MIRACLES

A. *Jesus and miracles*

1. Jesus was a man for others, never once thinking about himself. His miracles display this. Read these two miracles and then write a short summary paragraph telling how Jesus showed concern for others.

   Cure of the leper (Mk 1:40-45)
   Woman in the crowd (Lk 8:40-56)

2. Jesus was also sensitive to the individual. See this for yourself by reading:

   Blind Bartimaeus (Mk 10:46-52) Widow's son (Lk 7:11-17)

B. *Miracles today*

Remember the biblical definition of miracle. A miracle is a work of God which either demonstrates his power over the forces of evil or signifies God's love. A biblical definition of miracle is quite different from the idea of miracle as a suspension of the laws of nature. Given the biblical definition of miracle, discuss these questions:

1. Do miracles happen today? What do you think about Lourdes?
2. Can we work miracles in Jesus' name? Explain.
3. Have you ever witnessed a miracle? If so, why are you convinced that God was acting in this particular event?
4. Have you ever experienced a miracle of God's love or power, for example, a reformed alcoholic or drug addict? If so, share your experience.
5. Why might modern people not believe in miracles? Ask at least three Christian adults if they believe in miracles. Report back to class.

C. *The miracle of touch*

Did you notice how many of Jesus' miracles involve touching? Love flows through physical contact. As a matter of fact infants cannot survive unless they are fondled, cuddled, hugged, kissed and caressed very often. It is the only way they can experience love. Reflect here on your experience of touching others or being touched by them.

1. When was the last time your father or mother touched you? What did you *feel* at the time?
2. When was the last time you held a baby? What feelings did you have?
3. Do you touch your friends? How? Do you attribute any special meaning to your physical contact?
4. Are people today afraid to touch? Why or why not? If so, how do they show this fear?
5. Share one experience when the physical touch of another person was a true sign for you of God's love.
6. Keep track of how many people you touch in one day. Note what you do and the meaning behind it.

THE BOOK OF GLORY

The second part of John's gospel has been called the Book of Glory. There are three major divisions in the Book of Glory: the Last Supper (Jn 13-17), the passion and death of Jesus (Jn 18-19) and the resurrection (20). We will only briefly summarize some of the main themes from Jesus' Last Supper. The Last Supper discourse, as well as the passion and resurrection narratives, dramatically points to Jesus' triumph and the victory of salvation he has won for us.

Washing of the feet (Read Jn 13:1-17). John's gospel places the Last Supper a day earlier so that Jesus' death corresponds to the slaying of the Passover lambs. The lambs were sacrificed by the Jews to commemorate the Israelites' release from slavery in Egypt. In a more significant way Jesus—the Lamb of God—lays down his life so that all people can be freed from the slavery of sin. We commemorate Jesus' sacrifice every time we celebrate the Mass.

At this last meal with his disciples Jesus performed a parable-in-action. Peter knew only too well that not even a slave was required to perform such a menial task as washing the feet of another. He objected vigorously to Jesus' washing his feet. But Jesus wanted to teach his disciples that the way to glory was through service. All of us who want to follow our Lord are to take to heart these words: "If I, then, the Lord and Master, have washed your feet, you should wash each other's feet" (Jn 13:14). The Word-made-flesh demonstrated that the way of humility, suffering and service leads to the Father. The motto of a disciple of Jesus is be a footwasher.

Part 1 of the last discourse (Read Jn 14:1-31—this is substantially repeated in 16:4-33). Jesus teaches his disciples that he is the way, the truth and the life. We approach the Father through him. The Father and Jesus are one. Whatever we ask the Father in Jesus' name will be given to us.

In this section Jesus also promises to send the Holy Spirit, an advocate and protector. What is necessary is that we keep the Lord's commandments, especially the commandment to love one another. Love allows Jesus to dwell in us. Love brings peace. Love brings joy.

Part 2 of the last discourse (Read Jn 15:1-16:4).

> "A man can have no greater love
> than to lay down his life for his friends. . . .
> I call you friends" (Jn 15:13,15).

Here is the heart of the good news. Jesus does not call us slaves. He chose us as special people with the most important of all tasks: to love one another! He showed his love by dying for us. He continues to show his love by dwelling in us through the power of the Holy Spirit who will protect us and give us the courage to witness to Jesus and his truth. We are related to him as a vine is to its branches.

Consider the fact that Jesus calls us friends. What a powerful statement! He sees something tremendously worthwhile in each of us. He chose us to be his friends. Friends care for each other. They spend time together and share intimate thoughts. They sacrifice for each other. They accept each other unconditionally and love—even to death. Jesus demonstrated his love for his friends through his death. In return, he wants us to accept his love and friendship. He wants us to know in the core of our beings that we are loved. He wants us to discover that we do not have to be millionaires or extremely intelligent or terrifically beautiful or handsome to have his friendship. His friendship is a free gift which he gives. What he wants in return—simply—is our love:

> "What I command you
> is to love one another" (Jn 15:17).

These words are at the heart of the gospel call: to live a life of friendship with the Lord by loving one another.

Part 3 of the last discourse: Jesus' great prayer (Jn 17:1-26). This is one of the most beautiful passages in the New Testament. In this priestly prayer of Jesus, our Lord asks the Father to watch over us that we might be one with him and one with each other. It is a prayer of intercession for unity. United in community with the Holy Spirit, Jesus and the Father, we Christians are to glorify God by loving as the Lord loved.

Behind the words in this prayer is one of the great Christian truths: Jesus is active in the world today through Christians who are united to him. His gentle touch can be found in our hands. His forgiving words can be found on our lips. His passionate concern for others can be found in our kind deeds. His understanding can be found in our loving glances. The Lord lives in us. He can be found in the world today through us—people united to him. His Father is known through us. His message is heard only if we live it. This is the good news of salvation, but it is a tremendous responsibility for us to do what our Lord requires: Love.

A COUPLE OF REFLECTIONS

A. *Friendship and you.* What good news it is to have a friendship with the Lord. Friendship with anyone is precious, the most valuable gift we have. It demands time, work and some insight. In *The Friendship Factor* (Minneapolis: Augsburg Publishing House, 1979), Dr. Alan Loy McGinnis lists five helpful ways to deepen relationships with friends. They are listed below. Reflect on how well you are working at these in your relationships with your best friend and with Jesus. Use the following rating scale:

(5) I do this most of the time

(4) I usually do this

(3) Sometimes this reflects my relationship

(2) I do this infrequently

(1) I rarely do this

	Friend's Name: ____________	**Jesus**
1. I assign top priority to our relationship.	____	____
2. I am open and honest with my friend.	____	____
3. I talk about my affection. I tell my friend that I love him or her.	____	____
4. I practice the gestures of love. I break bread (eat) with my friend; I exchange gifts; I go out of my way for my friend.	____	____
5. I create space in my relationship; that is, I allow the other person his or her freedom. I don't cast my friend into my mold. I don't try to be superior or the center of attention.	____	____

Discuss:

1. Make and then discuss a list of practical ways each of the five factors above can be demonstrated in our relationship to our friend Jesus.

2. Discuss these sayings:

   "God gave us things to use and people to enjoy" (An old axiom).

   " 'Tis better to have loved and lost than never to have loved at all" (Tennyson).

   "We find ourselves by losing ourselves" (Jesus).

   "The meanest fear is the fear of sentimentality" (Chesterton).

B. *Footwashing.* To be a Christian leader means that we must serve as Jesus served; it means we must be willing to "wash feet." Make a list of three things you can do to "wash feet" in each of the following situations. Select four of these (one from each of the categories) and enact them during the next month or so. If the gospel is to come alive for others, it can only do so through you and your fellow Christians. Good deeds are an excellent way to show that Jesus lives.

At home

1. ______________________
____

2. ______________________
____

3. ______________________
____

At play

1. ______________________
____

2. ______________________
____

3. ______________________
____

At school

1. ______________________
____

2. ______________________
____

3. ______________________
____

At work

1. ______________________
____

2. ______________________
____

3. ______________________
____

SUMMARY

1. John's gospel presents the loftiest theology of the four gospels. John's Jesus is the Word of God, the light of the world who brings life, testifies to the truth and reveals the glory of God.

2. Scholars are unsure who finally penned the fourth gospel, though they tend to agree that the gospel is ultimately based on the witness of John, son of Zebedee, the beloved disciple.

3. John's gospel was written between 90 and 100 from Ephesus to a community of Christians who had been expelled from the Jewish synagogue. It was written to help people believe in Jesus. The gospel drew on three main sources: traditional material about Jesus, a signs source, and the passion narrative.

4. John differs from the synoptics in a number of ways. Characteristic of his gospel are long discourses of Jesus.

5. Gospel miracles show God's kingdom breaking into human history and indicate who Jesus is. They both require and strengthen faith. For John the miracles are signs that reveal God. John records seven of them. The raising of Lazarus brings together many of the themes of John's gospel: glory, light, misunderstanding, belief, resurrection, eternal life and the divinity of Jesus.

6. The first part of John's gospel is called the Book of Signs; the second part is referred to as the Book of Glory. Some of the important themes from the Book of Glory are Jesus is the Lamb of God who has come to serve; Jesus is the way, the truth and the life; and Jesus promises another Paraclete, the Holy Spirit. Jesus calls his friends to love as he has loved. Jesus prays that his followers might be one so that he can live through them and act in the world.

EVALUATION

Here are some quotes from the gospel of John. In a few sentences explain the significance of each quote, especially what the quote should mean to us today.

1. "The Word was made flesh and lived among us."

2. "There is the lamb of God that takes away the sin of the world."

3. "I am the bread of life."

4. "Love one another; just as I have loved you."

5. "I am the true vine."

READING GOD'S WORD

For the last few chapters you have been reading about the adventures of Paul in Acts. The rest of Acts (21:17-28:31) tells of Paul's further adventures. He goes to Jerusalem after returning from his third missionary journey and is accused by the Jews there of profaning the Temple. He is arrested, defends himself before the Jews and the Sanhedrin and narrowly escapes with his life. He is transferred to Caesarea where Felix, the Roman procurator, hears his case. Felix keeps Paul under house arrest for two years.

After the two years a new procurator, Festus, hears Paul's case. So does King Agrippa who is somewhat sympathetic to Paul. Because Paul as a Roman citizen appeals for a hearing before Caesar, he is sent to Rome. He has an exciting journey, braving a hurricane and becoming shipwrecked on the island of Malta where he cures many people. When he finally arrives in Rome, he makes contact with the Roman Jews and continues to preach the good news of Jesus. He is imprisoned there from 61 to 63. Acts ends on a triumphant note with Paul openly preaching God's kingdom.

To finish Paul's story: Paul was eventually set free for lack of evidence. Later he was again imprisoned. Tradition has it that he was executed by beheading in Rome around 67.

Read some of these further adventures of Paul and answer the questions below.

Read Acts 22:1-21.

1. Where was Paul born? ______________________________

2. Who was his teacher? ______________________________

3. Where was Paul when Jesus appeared to him a second time?

____

What mission did the Lord give to him? ____________________

Read Acts 24:1-10.

4. What charges did the Jews bring against Paul?

___

Read Acts 26:24-32.

5. What was Festus' opinion of Paul?

___

6. What did King Agrippa think of Paul?

___

7. Why was Paul sent to Rome?

___

Read Acts 27.

8. Why were the occupants of the boat spared their lives?

___

Read Acts 28.

9. What two marvelous things did Paul do in Malta?

___

___

10. Was Paul successful in preaching to the Jews in Rome?

___

Why/or why not? ___

PRAYER REFLECTION

Darken the room. Light a candle to represent the presence of Jesus Christ, the light of the world. Reflectively and quietly put yourself in the presence of the Lord and the light of his love. Feel the warmth of that love. After a few moments, have one person slowly and meditatively read the following excerpts from Jesus' Priestly Prayer (Jn 17:1-26). Think of what is being said. Consider the responsibility that our Lord gives to you. Thank him for his love.

"Father, the hour has come:
glorify your Son
so that your Son may glorify you;
and, through the power over all mankind that you have given him,
let him give eternal life to all those you have entrusted to him.
And eternal life is this:
to know you,
the only true God,
and Jesus Christ whom you have sent. . . .

Holy Father,
keep those you have given me true to your name,
so that they may be one like us.
While I was with them,
I kept those you had given me true to your name.
I have watched over them and not one is lost
except the one who chose to be lost,
and this was to fulfill the scriptures.
But now I am coming to you
and while still in the world I say these things
to share my joy with them to the full.
I passed your word on to them,
and the world hated them,
because they belong to the world
no more than I belong to the world.
I am not asking you to remove them from the world,
but to protect them from the evil one. . . .
As you sent me into the world,
I have sent them into the world,
and for their sake I consecrate myself

so that they too may be consecrated in truth.
I pray not only for these,
but for those also
who through their words will believe in me.
May they all be one. . . .

Father, Righteous One,
the world has not known you,
but I have known you,
and these have known
that you have sent me.
I have made your name known to them
and will continue to make it known,
so that the love with which you loved me may be in them,
and so that I may be in them."

7
The Letters of St. Paul

> All I can say is that I forget the past and I strain ahead for what is still to come; I am racing for the finish, for the prize to which God calls us upwards to receive in Christ Jesus.
>
> —Philippians 3:13-14

One of the most compelling figures in the New Testament is St. Paul. You have already read about his exploits in the Acts of the Apostles.

Paul was born around A.D. 10. He was a Jew of the tribe of Benjamin and probably received a good Greek education. He lived a strict Jewish life and studied to be a rabbi. In his early career he was notorious for persecuting Christians. This changed when our Lord appeared to him, probably in the year 36. He was baptized and then spent some time in the Arabian desert.

Roughly three years after his conversion Paul went to Jerusalem and conferred with the authorities there. He returned to his hometown and around 44 went to Antioch to work with Barnabas. He labored there for a year. The church in Antioch sent him and Barnabas to Jerusalem to help the Christians there during a famine.

Between 46 and 48 Paul, along with Barnabas and John Mark, engaged in a first missionary journey which took him from Cyprus through southern Galatia. He returned to Jerusalem in 49 for the first council of the church.

Paul's second journey (A.D. 49-52) began on a note of controversy with Barnabas over John Mark. Paul and Barnabas went their separate ways. Paul's journey took him to Europe where he crossed into Macedonia and Greece. Along the way he was ably assisted by Timothy.

The third journey spanned the years 53 to 57. Paul spent considerable time in Ephesus. He returned to Jerusalem in 58 and was imprisoned. He was later moved to Caesarea where he was put under house arrest for two years. After several hearings before the authorities Paul was dispatched to Rome where he was kept under house arrest for two more years awaiting a trial. He was finally let go for lack of evidence against him. Tradition tells us that Paul was arrested again under the persecution of Nero and finally put to death in the year 67.

Besides living this adventurous life in spreading the good news of Jesus, Paul wrote letters or *epistles* to bolster the faith of the communities he evangelized. The New Testament contains 21 of these epistles, 13 of which were either written by or are attributed to Paul. Unlike personal letters intended for only one person, New Testament epistles were meant to be read and reflected on by the entire community.

New Testament letters have a common form. There is 1) *an opening formula* which gives the name of the sender and the receiver and a short greeting. The opening is followed by 2) *a thanksgiving* which sets the tone of the letter and for Paul is often prayerful and gives a hint about the content of the letter. The body of the letter follows the thanksgiving. Here is found 3) *the message* of the epistle. Paul's letters usually have two parts to the message: a doctrinal section which discusses the truths of the Christian message and a hortatory section which gives encouragement and instruction on how to live a good Christian life. New Testament letters end with 4) *a conclusion and a final greeting.* This last section often contains personal news and specific advice given to individuals in the community for whom the letter is written. Paul's final greeting is often a blessing that goes like this: "The grace of our Lord Jesus Christ be with you" (1 Thes 5:28).

This chapter will briefly summarize the letters of Paul in the order in which they were probably written. Seven of the 13 letters attributed to Paul were definitely written by him: Romans, 1 and 2 Corinthians, 1 Thessalonians, Galatians, Philippians and Philemon. Scholars cannot say for sure that 2 Thessalonians, Ephesians, Colossians, 1 and 2 Timothy and Titus were written by Paul. They may have been composed by secretaries or disciples of Paul who wrote in his name and reflected his preaching and teaching.

In your New Testament you will note that the letters are not arranged in chronological order. Paul's letters are collected into two groups. The first group includes these epistles sent to various churches; they are arranged in order of length from longest to shortest. Romans, being the longest, is first, and 2 Thessalonians is last because it is the shortest in this group. The second group contains letters addressed to individuals. 1 Timothy is listed first in this group because it is the longest and Philemon is listed last because it is the shortest.

You will read some of Paul's letters in their entirety. Others will be summarized. In still others, you will read key chapters which treat some of the major themes of Paul's message. These themes flow from Paul's profound personal relationship with Jesus Christ. For Paul, Jesus is both a living Lord and friend who is intimately concerned with everyone. The Lord is present in a special way through his body, the church. We Christians are united to Jesus in a deep and personal way. Here is a summary of the themes of Paul's letters.

1. Salvation takes place through Jesus Christ, the Lord of the universe.
2. The heart of the gospel is the death and resurrection of Jesus.
3. We will participate in the resurrection of Jesus Christ.
4. Salvation is a free gift of God that demands faith. We cannot earn it.
5. We Christians are bound together in one body, the church, of which Jesus is the head.

6. The Holy Spirit is the life of the church who enables us to call God Abba.
7. The brothers and sisters of Jesus should treat each other with dignity. We must love.
8. Following Jesus means that we must suffer for him gladly.

PAUL, THE APOSTLE FOR CHRIST

You have read a lot about Paul in the Acts of the Apostles. Test your knowledge of his life by taking this short quiz. Circle the correct answer. Check your answers with the citations at the end.

1. Paul was born in a. Antioch; b. Jerusalem; c. Tarsus; d. Damascus; e. Caesarea
2. Paul was a(n) a. Pharisee; b. Sadducee; c. Essene; d. Zealot
3. Paul was converted on the road to a. Jerusalem; b. Damascus; c. Antioch; d. Capernaum
4. Paul made his living as a a. weaver; b. tent-maker; c. carpenter; d. camel-driver
5. Paul's famous teacher was a. Hillel; b. Shammai; c. Jonathan ben Zacchai; d. Gamaliel
6. Paul was baptized by a. Stephen; b. Ananias; c. Peter; d. James; e. Barnabas
7. As a Roman citizen, Paul was taken to Rome because he appealed to a. the Roman governor; b. the Christians there; c. Caesar; d. the Senate.

Answers

1. Acts 22:3
2. Acts 23:6
3. Acts 9:3
4. Acts 18:3
5. Acts 22:3
6. Acts 9:17-19
7. Acts 25:12

CHRONOLOGICAL DISCUSSION OF PAUL'S LETTERS

1 and 2 Thessalonians

Background. Thessalonika was an important crossroads town, a commercial center and the capital of the Roman province of Macedonia. Paul visited this city of 70,000 inhabitants during his second missionary journey, probably in the year 50. With co-workers Timothy and Silas, Paul preached the gospel first to the Jews in their synagogues and then to the "God-fearing" Gentiles. He made some converts there, thus raising the ire of the Jewish community. A public uproar resulted, and Paul and his companions fled at night to Beroea. After a short visit there Paul travelled to Athens and eventually to Corinth for an extended stay.

While at Corinth Paul became concerned about the community at Thessalonika which he had been forced to leave. He sent Timothy back to the city to find out what was going on. Timothy's report to Paul occasioned the writing of Paul's first epistles.

1 Thessalonians. This letter was written from Corinth in 51. It is a simple letter. Note the four-part division:

- 1:1 The address (opening formula)
- 1:3-10 The initial thanksgiving
- 2:1-5:22 The message
  - 2:1-3:13 Paul's expressions of personal concern for the Thessalonians and his thanksgiving for them
  - 4:1-5:22 Paul's instructions and encouragement to the community
- 5:23-28 Conclusion and final greeting

In the second part of the message section (4:1-5:22) Paul responds to some of the concerns which emerged from Timothy's visit. First, Paul reminds his recent converts that Christians are called to holiness. They must live loving and sexually pure lives. Second, Paul wants to reassure the Thessalonians who were concerned about the fate of their friends who died before the Lord's second coming. Would they lose their share in the coming glory? Paul tells them that both the living and the dead shall rise with Christ when he comes again. He reminds them that no one knows for sure when the Lord will return so that they should always be watchful as they await his return.

The letter ends with Paul reminding his converts to live a life of peace and love in community.

2 Thessalonians. This second letter, also written from Corinth in 51 quickly followed the first one. Apparently Paul received word that the Thessalonians were very confused about the Lord's second coming. This confusion led to some Thessalonians refusing to work. Their reasoning probably went like this: Why bother to work if the world is going to end soon?

After an initial address and thanksgiving, Paul writes that at the Last Judgment God will punish those who have persecuted Christians (1:5-10). This is followed by Paul's prayer for the Thessalonians to be faithful (1:11-12).

Chapter 2 of the letter discusses the second coming of Jesus. Paul says that the second coming has not happened because certain signs have not yet taken place. He once again calls for perseverance and prayer.

Just as it looks as though Paul is going to end his letter (3:1-5), he interrupts himself and takes up the issue of the non-workers. He gives some rather stern advice before he writes—in his own hand—his final greetings.

Read 2 Thessalonians and answer the following questions:

1:3-12 Why does Paul expect Christians to suffer?________________

____

For class discussion:

1. How do young people today suffer for their belief in Jesus? Give examples.
2. How do we glorify "our Lord Jesus Christ" (1:12) by the good things we do?

2:1-3:5 List two things that Paul says must happen before Christ comes a second time: a. ______________________

b. ______________________

Where are we Christians to get the strength to resist the temptations of the evil one?

For class discussion:

3. Is it a good idea for Christians to try to identify a particular historical person with the enemy? Why or why not?
4. Should we worry about the end of the world? Why or why not?

3:5-18 What's Paul's attitude to those who aren't working? ______

____

How do we know that this letter belongs to Paul? __________

____

For class discussion:

5. Do you agree with Paul's advice about Christians who aren't pulling their own weight?

Extra Reading for Review: You may wish to reread about Paul's visit to Thessalonika and his escape to Beroea. If so, take a look at Acts 17:1-15.

Galatians

Background. Paul's letter to the Galatians is an angry letter that does two major things: 1) It defends Paul's right to teach the gospel; and 2) It corrects the errors of some false teachers who claimed that Gentiles must become Jews first before becoming Christians.

Galatians was addressed to a group of churches—Iconium, Derbe and Lystra—all cities in the Roman province of Galatia which Paul had visited both on his second and third journeys. It was probably written while Paul stayed at Ephesus (A.D. 54-57), though scholars cannot tell for sure if it was written before or after 1 Corinthians.

In this letter Paul first defends his right to teach the gospel. Some false teachers claimed that Paul had no right to teach since Paul was not one of the original apostles. On his visit to Galatia Paul had taught that the Jewish law does not save a person. Only faith in Jesus Christ brings salvation. In two autobiographical sections (1:11-24 and 2:1-10) Paul defends his teaching. He reminds the Galatians of his divine call to teach and that the apostles in Jerusalem, led by Peter, agree with his teaching.

Second, Paul defends what he preached. Since Jesus' coming Christians were freed from the need to be circumcised and to follow all 613 laws of the Jewish Torah. False teachers were trying to sway the Galatians into thinking that by strictly following the Jewish law, they would meet the demands of the gospel. Paul taught that faith in Jesus—not following 613 laws—brings salvation. Faith in Jesus forces a person to be responsible and decide to do the right thing with the guidance of the Holy Spirit. The Law served a purpose before Jesus, but with the coming of the Spirit, Christians were called to freedom and responsibility; they are to be governed by the law of love.

Galatians is perhaps the sharpest letter Paul ever wrote. His initial address (1:1-5) is not very friendly at all. He omits his usual prayer of thanksgiving and instead issues a warning to his readers (1:6-10). The doctrinal section of the letter defends his apostleship and his preaching of the gospel and teaches about faith (1:11-4:31). The hortatory section teaches how Christians should live when guided by the Holy Spirit (5:1-6:10). The letter concludes with an epilogue and a final blessing (6:11-18).

Read Galatians 3-6 and answer the following questions:

3:1-22 What attitude does Paul have toward the Galatians?

____

____

According to Paul, what was the purpose of the Law?

____

____

3:29-4:31 What makes us children of God?

____

What makes us one in the Lord?

____

What allegory does Paul use to stress the fact that Christians are called to freedom?

____

____

5-6 Faith must express itself in ________________.

Name six things self-indulgence brings:

a. ________________ b. ________________

c. ________________ d. ________________

e. ________________ f. ________________

Name six things the Spirit brings:

a. ________________ b. ________________

c. ________________ d. ________________

e. ________________ f. ________________

What does Paul think of circumcision?

____

____

What is important for him?

____

____

For class discussion:

1. Does Christian freedom mean that we can do whatever we want to do? Why or why not?
2. Christian freedom means we are free to serve others. Do you agree? Why or why not?

For Reflection: Galatians 5:22-23 lists the fruits or gifts of the Holy Spirit. How do you measure up to them? Rate yourself on how well these gifts are manifested in your life by marking the appropriate number in the space provided. Then give one example of how you can live each gift of the Spirit either at home or at school.

1—this describes me well

2—this usually describes me

3—I'm a bit weak on this virtue

4—I need lots of work on this Christian virtue

GIFTS	*RATING*	*EXAMPLE*
loving	___	______________________
		______________________
joyful	___	______________________
		______________________
peaceful	___	______________________
		______________________
patient	___	______________________
		______________________
kind	___	______________________
		______________________
good	___	______________________
		______________________
trustworthy	___	______________________
		______________________
gentle	___	______________________
		______________________
self-controlled	___	______________________
		______________________

1 and 2 Corinthians

Background. Corinth was considered the "sin city" of the ancient world. As a thriving port it attracted all kinds of people and philosophies. It was the center of worship to the goddess Aphrodite. Worship to her involved temple prostitution. In fact, the term *Corinthian maiden* meant "prostitute."

From both Acts and Paul's letters we learn that Paul visited Corinth three times. He had a particularly difficult time with the Christians there. As soon as he left the first time, the church there broke into many rival factions. Bizarre beliefs and practices sprang up. Paul's letters were primarily written to correct the abuses which had crept into the Corinthian church.

Although we now have only two of the letters Paul wrote to Corinth, he probably wrote four of them. The first letter was written shortly after his first visit (Acts 18:1-18) and probably warned the Corinthian Christians not to associate with immoral Christians. This letter is now lost. The Corinthian church responded to Paul's letter, and this response, which raised many questions for Paul to answer, caused Paul to write still another letter. This letter is our 1 Corinthians.

However, the conflicts were not resolved, so Paul went to Corinth for a visit (Acts 20:1-3). He had a bad time there on his second visit and was forced to write a third, very severe letter. This letter is also lost, though sections of it may appear in 2 Corinthians. Worried about how his converts might react to his sharp letter, Paul decided to visit Corinth a third time (see 2 Cor 13:1). On the way to Corinth Paul received good news about the church there from Titus and then decided to send a more cheerful, peacemaking letter. This fourth letter is our 2 Corinthians.

1 Corinthians. This letter was probably written from Ephesus during Paul's third missionary journey. Scholars date it between the years 55 and 57. The letter takes up a number of problems and issues which had been troubling the Corinthian church. Some of these problems were rival factions in the Corinthian church, challenges to Paul's authority, Christians submitting their disputes to pagan courts, various scandals, what to do about marriage and virginity, what to do about meat offered to idols, disorders in the assembly when celebrating the Eucharist, the nature of spiritual gifts, and doubts about the resurrection from the dead.

1 Corinthians has a customary opening formula (1:1-3) and prayer of thanksgiving (1:4-9). The message is broken into four main topics:

1. *Splits in the Corinthian church* (1:10-4:21). Faith in Jesus is more important than the wisdom and knowledge so highly prized by the Greek Corinthians.
2. *Problems in Christian living* (5:1-11:1). Paul deals with the issue of legal disputes among Christians, with problems of sex and marriage, with that to do about eating meat offered to idols and with the issue of Christian freedom.
3. *Problems in Christian worship* (11:2-14:40). Paul stresses the theme of unity among Christians, highlighting the image of Christ's body. Divisions when worshipping have no place for Christians.
4. *Belief in the resurrection* (15:1-58). Paul clears up some false beliefs about the resurrection. Along the way, he quotes the earliest Christian creed about the resurrection of Jesus (15:3-8).

The conclusion discusses collections for the needy and includes many personal greetings (16:1-24).

Sampling 1 Corinthians. Here are some passages which deal with Paul's solutions to some of the problems in the Corinthian church. Read them and answer the questions.

1. *Factions in the church* (Read 1 Cor 1:10-16; 3:1-15). What does Paul think of the Corinthian slogans?

____

____

____

____

2. *Problem of incest* (Read 1 Cor 5). What was the nature of the problem and what is Paul's solution?

____

____

____

____

3. *Legal disputes* (Read 1 Cor 6:1-8). How should Christians settle their legal disputes?

____

____

____

____

4. *Fornication* (Read 1 Cor 6:12-20). What is fornication? Why is it wrong for Christians?

____

____

____

____

5. *Problems with celebrating the Eucharist* (Read 1 Cor 11:17-34). What was going on at Corinth? Why was it wrong?

____

____

____

____

6. *Problem with spiritual gifts* (Read 1 Cor 12-14). Why does God give different gifts?

What analogy does Paul use?

What is the most important gift and why?

Class project: Make a list of problems which are present in your parish. Construct a letter, similar in style to Paul's, which addresses these various problems.

Discuss: 1. Is it proper for a pastor to correct the faults he finds in his congregation? Why or why not?
2. How does Paul understand the church?

2 Corinthians. Paul also wrote this letter between 55 and 57 from somewhere in Macedonia. Paul was distressed to learn that some other missionaries who followed him to Corinth had been causing trouble. Like the false teachers who had infiltrated the churches in Galatia, they were telling Christians that the way to salvation was by following Jewish customs and laws rather than believing in Jesus. These false teachers were given the name Judaizers.

Paul probably met these false teachers on his second trip to Corinth. An unpleasant confrontation resulted. Back in Ephesus, he wrote the lost third letter. He severely criticized these teachers because they misled a number of his Corinthian converts. He decided to visit Corinth again, but before going there he wished to smooth things over. 2 Corinthians is Paul's attempt to set things right before his visit.

In the main section of 2 Corinthians Paul does the following:

1. Talks about his impending trip to Corinth (1:12-2:17).
2. Defends his own teaching ministry (3:1-6:10).
3. Appeals to the Corinthians' good nature and consoles them (6:11-7:16).
4. Talks about the collection for the church in Jerusalem (8-9).
5. Sarcastically and strongly defends himself against the attacks of the false teachers (10:1-13:10).

Certain sections of 2 Corinthians may contain earlier letters of Paul; for example, 2 Corinthians 6:14-7:1 may be part of Paul's very first letter written to the Corinthians (before 1 Corinthians) and 2 Corinthians 10-13 may well be part of the third, harshly worded letter sent shortly before 2 Corinthians.

Read 2 Corinthians 10-13.

Read Paul's defense and discuss what kind of person he was. Do you admire him?

Romans

Background. Unlike many of Paul's other letters, Romans was written to a church not established by Paul. He intended to pass through Rome on his way to Spain, a trip he probably did not make because of his arrest in Jerusalem after his third journey. This—the longest of Paul's letters—is a letter of introduction to the Romans. By the time Paul wrote it (A.D. 56-58) he was well aware of some of the attacks false teachers (Judaizers) made about his teaching. Thus Paul constructed a clear, highly developed *theological letter* spelling out his beliefs to the Romans.

The theme of the letter is clearly stated:

> For I am not ashamed of the Good News: it is the power of God saving all who have faith—Jews first, but Greeks as well—since this is what reveals the justice of God to us: it shows how faith leads to faith, or as scripture says: *The upright man finds life through faith* (Rom 1:16-17).

In the letter Paul was trying to do two things: He was trying to show that Greek (Gentile) dependence on *knowledge* of right and wrong does not save a person. Only faith in Jesus saves. At the same time he was trying to show that the Jewish dependence on the *Law* and Jewish customs does not save a person either. Only faith in Jesus saves. These same points appear in Paul's letter to the Galatians. Paul gives them more detailed treatment in Romans.

Outline. The message of Romans has two major divisions, a doctrinal section (1:16-11:35) and a Christian living part (12:1-15:13). The doctrinal part stresses that despite unbelief in both Gentiles and Jews, God still graciously offers his salvation to all people. This loving salvation conquers sin because of Jesus and brings true justice, a justice where God reconciles all people to himself through *faith* in Jesus Christ. The Christian living part stresses that faith in Jesus leads to a life of love. Christians must be humble, love even enemies, obey proper authority, avoid bad example, forgive, act as one, and the like. In short, faith in Jesus means Christians will love as he did.

Because of the difficulty of Romans, here is a topical outline of the letter:

1. *The human condition* (1:18-3:20). Paul shows that sin pervades human history. The Gentiles, using their human reason, should have discovered God, but instead they worshipped creation instead of the Creator (1:18-2:16). The Jews should have been better off because they had the Law. But they did not keep it. Both Jews and Gentiles are under the power of sin (2:17-3:20).
2. *Faith in Jesus saves* (3:21-31). Neither knowledge nor Law saves. God's free gift of grace alone saves. Jesus' death brings salvation to both Jew and Gentile.
3. *Abraham: example of faith* (4:1-25). Paul cites Abraham as the key example of faith. Abraham's attitude must be our attitude.
4. *God's salvation and human freedom* (5-8). Jesus is the new Adam who has brought eternal life to us (chapter 5). Faith and baptism in the Lord accomplish what the law could not—they free us from the power of sin (chapter 6). Faith frees the Christian from Jewish law (chapter 7). We are children of God by power of the Holy Spirit. His new life in us unites us totally to God's love (chapter 8).

5. *God will remain faithful to the Jews* (9-11). The Jews do not seem to be accepting God's salvation. But God's promises to Israel stand, and he will eventually melt their hearts.
6. *Christian living* (12-15). Freedom in faith demands responsible Christian living, living based on love.

Read Romans 5-8.

Write a short summary of each chapter in the space provided.

Chapter 5

____

____

____

Chapter 6

____

____

____

Chapter 7

____

____

____

Chapter 8

____

____

____

____

For Reflection:

1. *Comment:* "With God on our side who can be against us?" (Rom 8:31). "Nothing therefore can come between us and the love of Christ, even if we are troubled or worried, or being persecuted, or lacking food or clothes, or being threatened or even attacked" (Rom 8:35).

2. In Romans 7:14-25 Paul talks about the struggle we all have in doing the right thing. We make good intentions but so easily fail in following them. Can you think of five good things you wished to do recently but didn't follow through on?

   a. ______________________________

   b. ______________________________

   c. ______________________________

   d. ______________________________

   e. ______________________________

   Does this discourage you or make you see even more the need for our Lord's help?

PAUL AND THE ROMAN WORLD

To get to know Paul's world better, prepare a short report for the class on one of these research topics:

1. *Roman philosophies.* Read in more depth about one of the popular philosophies of Paul's day. Examples: Gnosticism, Epicureanism, Stoicism.
2. *Prison Life.* What was it like to be a prisoner in the Roman world in the first century?
3. *Emperors.* Who were the Roman emperors from A.D. 10 to 67? What were their major achievements? What was their attitude to new religions?

Captivity Letters: Philippians, Philemon, Colossians, Ephesians

Introduction. Philippians, Philemon, Colossians and Ephesians are often grouped together and termed Captivity Letters. They get this name because they were written while the author was in prison. Philippians, though, is usually considered separately for two reasons: 1) Many scholars today believe that the letter was sent from Ephesus

around the year 56 or 57 rather than from Rome (in 62 or 63) as had been thought for centuries; and 2) the theology of this epistle seems to be closer to the "great" letters of Paul: Romans, Galatians, and 1 and 2 Corinthians.

Philemon, Colossians and Ephesians, on the other hand, have more in common. They all seem to have been written while Paul was imprisoned in Rome between 61 and 63. They were entrusted to one messenger, Tychicus (Eph 6:21 and Col 4:7). Their theological content and style of writing are also very close.

Philippians. Philippi was a Roman military colony; its population was made up of many army veterans. Paul visited the city three times: during his second missionary journey in 50, during the third journey in 57, and on his way back from Corinth in 58. Paul loved the Philippians in a special way; it was the only community from which he would receive any material aid for his mission. Many scholars today believe that Philippians is a composite of three short letters written by Paul to the community.

Paul wrote this letter to thank the Philippians for the gift which they sent to him (Phil 4:14-18) and to thank them for sending along the bearer of the gift, Epaphroditus, who had fallen ill and risked much for the sake of Paul and the gospel (Phil 2:25-29).

The word *rejoice* is used many times as Paul teaches about Christian living—the need for harmony, peace and humility, and the need to die and rise with Christ. Doctrinally the heart of the letter is the hymn to Christ which appears in Philippians 2:6-11. There Paul praises the humility of Christ who became man so that we can win salvation. We must adore the Lord who has done so much for us.

Read Philippians.

Do the following:

Chapter 1: Does Paul fear death? Why or why not? ____________

____

Paul considers not only believing in Christ a privilege, but also ______________________________ for him.

Chapter 2: Summarize the hymn to Christ (Phil 2:6-11) in your own words.

____

____

____

What athletic image does Paul use to describe his mission?__________________ Is this a good image? Discuss.

Chapter 3: What does the term *cutters* refer to? ____________

Does Paul use this term in a positive or a negative way? Why or why not?

____

____

How are we supposed to attain Christian perfection?

____

Chapter 4: Which churches have helped Paul with material aid?

____

Discuss: Here is some practical advice from Philippians. Discuss what you think Paul means.

1. "Always consider the other person to be better than yourself" (Phil 2:3).
2. Paul asks the Philippians to model their lives on those who are living a good Christian life. Is this good advice? Who do you think is worth modeling today? Refer to Philippians 3:17.

Philemon. You have already read this short letter. Paul, writing from Rome, advises Philemon to accept back with forgiveness his runaway slave, Onesimus. The letter emphasizes the true dignity of Christians who, because they are united to Christ, must love one another. Paul does not condemn slavery as such in the letter. Rather, he pleads with Philemon to accept Onesimus with kindness and suggests that he might free him and send him back to Paul to help with his mission. This letter was written entirely in Paul's own hand and was sent to Philemon at Colossae.

Colossians. Colossae was a textile town located in a river valley around 110 miles east of Ephesus. Epaphras established the church there. Paul received word of some dangerous heresies which had infected the community in Ephesus. The people believed in astrology, the belief that stars controlled people's fate. Paul warns against this in Colossians 2:8,20. There was also a belief that certain angelic beings controlled human affairs, even creation itself. This strange belief, which came from paganism and some branches of Judaism, tended to put Christ in a secondary place. Paul strongly warns against this tendency, saying that with Christ no one else is needed. All the fullness of God and his power is in Jesus Christ (Col 1:19; 2:3,9); Christ—not some intermediate beings—is Lord of the universe.

Some scholars suggest a very close disciple of Paul wrote this letter in his name. The outline of the letter looks like this:

1. Introduction (Greetings, thanksgiving, prayer) 1:1-12
2. Doctrine 1:13-3:4
    a. Christ is pre-eminent in the universe and the church 1:13-2:3
    b. Warnings against false teachers 2:4-3:4
3. The Christian life 3:5-4:1
4. Conclusion 4:2-18

Read Colossians.

Make a list of six separate verses where Paul clearly states that Jesus Christ is supreme. Write out the verses. Also, list five verses which contain some practical advice on the Christian life which is especially meaningful to you. Share these with the class and discuss your choices for Christian living.

Christ is supreme	*Practical advice*
1. ______	1. ______
2. ______	2. ______
3. ______	3. ______
4. ______	4. ______
5. ______	5. ______
6. ______	

Ephesians. Ephesians is closely related in its message to Colossians. Just as Romans developed more fully the thought contained in Galatians, so does Ephesians expand the doctrine of Colossians.

Ephesians may well have been a circular letter—one that was meant to be read in many different churches. One of Paul's disciples may have written this epistle approximately at the time when Paul was imprisoned in Rome.

The theme of the letter is unity in Christ. Christ redeems all people, reconciles them and calls them into oneness with the Father, Son and Holy Spirit. Like most of Paul's letters Ephesians contains a doctrinal section and practical advice on Christian living.

Read the following short passage from Ephesians in which Paul encourages Christians to arm themselves like Roman soldiers to battle for the Lord. Note the images he uses.

Read Ephesians 6:14-17.

The Pastoral Letters: 1 and 2 Timothy and Titus

If Paul actually wrote these three letters, he probably wrote them between 65 and 67 sometime after his first arrest in Rome. 1 Timothy and Titus may have been written from someplace in Macedonia, while 2 Timothy would have been written in 67 shortly before Paul's execution in Rome. These letters are called pastoral because they were written by one pastor (Paul) and sent to two pastors (Timothy and Titus), both close disciples of Paul.

Scholarly opinion today, though, judges that these three letters were most probably written at the turn of the first century, and that authorship was attributed to Paul.

Addressed to individuals rather than to particular communities, the purpose of the three letters is to give concrete directions on how to organize and administer the local churches. Timothy, an early convert and companion of Paul, presided over the church at Ephesus. Titus, also a convert of Paul and a companion with him to the Council of Jerusalem, headed the church in Crete.

The letters deal with the following concerns:

1. The author wants sound doctrine taught and the deposit of faith guarded. Like many of the early Christian communities, the churches of Timothy and Titus were plagued by heretics who were spreading false teaching. Some of these teachers

were similar to the Judaizers; others reflected a kind of gnosticism which distrusted the material world and forbade marriage and the eating of certain foods. The author claims that these teachers taught for financial gain.

2. These letters are concerned about church organization. They contain rules about how church officials should be appointed and regulations on how worship is supposed to take place.

3. Finally, these letters, like all of Paul's epistles, give many instructions on how Christians should live a life worthy of their vocation in Christ.

Read 1 Timothy.

Discuss the following questions:

Chapter 1: What theme(s) do you see emerging in this chapter which concerned Paul in some of his earlier letters?

Chapter 2: Do Paul's recommendations about women at church make sense today? Why or why not?

Chapter 3: Comment on Paul's list of recommendations for the elder-in-charge. What would you add or subtract today? Should today's priests be allowed to marry?

Chapter 4: Paul says that everything God created is good (1 Tm 4:4). What makes the use of a created good wrong? Give some examples.

Chapters 5 and 6: Comment on some of the practical advice Paul gives in these chapters. Is the advice still worthwhile today? Explain.

SUMMARY

1. Thirteen epistles are attributed to Paul or his close disciples. New Testament epistles were meant to be read publicly. They contain an opening formula, a thanksgiving, a message usually with both doctrine and practical advice, and a conclusion.

2. The earliest letters written by Paul were 1 and 2 Thessalonians. They encourage his recent converts and give instructions about the second coming of the Lord.

3. Galatians, Romans, and 1 and 2 Corinthians are considered the greatest of Paul's letters because of their length and the theological content contained in them. Galatians gives a spirited defense of Paul's ministry. Romans develops more elaborately Paul's teaching on faith and its relationship to salvation, a theme discussed first in Galatians. 1 and 2 Corinthians deal with some difficult problems that faced a rather unruly congregation—issues of belief and issues of practical morality.

4. Philippians, Philemon, Colossians and Ephesians are called the Captivity Letters. Philippians contains a wonderful hymn to Christ and exhibits much joy for a community Paul obviously loved. Philemon contains instructions on how the recipient of the letter should treat his slave. Colossians and Ephesians both warn against false teachers and stress the preeminence of Jesus Christ.

5. The Pastoral Letters include 1 and 2 Timothy, and Titus. They take up many practical concerns of church organization and government. They also stress the need for pastors to teach sound doctrine.

6. The major themes of Paul's epistles can be summarized as follows:

a. Salvation takes place through Jesus Christ, the Lord of the universe.

b. The heart of the gospel is the death and resurrection of Jesus.

c. We will participate in the resurrection of Jesus Christ.

d. Salvation is a free gift of God that demands faith. We cannot earn it.

e. We Christians are bound together in one body, the church, of which Jesus is the head.
f. The Holy Spirit is the life of the church who enables us to call God Abba.
g. Brothers and sisters of Jesus should treat each other with dignity. We must love.
h. Following Jesus means that we must suffer for him gladly.

EVALUATION

Read the following eight passages from Paul's epistles. Using the list of themes given in No. 6 of the Summary (page 223), match each reading with a theme. Mark the letter of the theme in the space provided. Each of the letters is used only once.

____	Rom 8:31-39	____	1 Cor 15:20-28
____	Gal 4:1-7	____	Col 1:15-20
____	Eph 4:17-32	____	2 Thes 1:3-5
____	Gal 3:23-29	____	1 Cor 12:12-30

READING GOD'S WORD

No one knows for sure who wrote the letter to the Hebrews. For a long time people thought that Paul wrote it. Today most scholars conclude that the author is not Paul because the theology, language and style of Hebrews differ so dramatically from Paul's other letters.

Hebrews, probably written in the 80s, reads like a lofty sermon. It is a difficult letter that attempts to encourage the faith of Christians who are undergoing persecution. Using a lot of Old Testament references, Hebrews attempts to show that Jesus is the supreme High Priest, the most important mediator between God and his people. Jesus perfectly fulfills the ancient promises made to the Jews.

The climax to the letter can be found in chapter 12 where Jesus is presented as the prime example of one who fulfills the Father's will. We Christians are encouraged to follow his example. Sample this letter by reading the following passages:

Hebrews 1-2 Jesus, God's total revelation

Hebrews 4:12-5:12 Jesus, God's Word and High Priest

Hebrews 11-12:4 Examples of people who kept faith

PRAYER REFLECTION

Lord, your apostle Paul said it so well . . .
"Help me run the good race."

It is you, Lord, who gives me the strength to keep going.

It is you, Lord, who calls me to victory.

I ask you to give me the fierce determination of Paul
to do the right thing even if others mock me
to suffer for you quietly and cheerfully
to love even those I find difficult to love.

Arm me with truth, patience and kindness.

If you help me, Lord, I know I'll make it.
With you on my side, who can be against me?
Amen . . . and thanks, Lord.

8
Other New Testament Writings and Conclusion

God is love
and anyone who lives in love lives in God,
and God lives in him.
—1 John 4:16

This chapter brings us to the end of our introduction to the writings of the New Testament. In it, we will take a brief look at the last book of the Bible, the book of Revelation, and then we will study a group of seven epistles which are known as the Catholic Epistles. The term *catholic* in this context refers to the "general" nature of these seven works; they were generally sent to a number of churches in a wide area. This is in contrast to most of Paul's letters which were addressed to particular or individual churches. These letters include James; 1 and 2 Peter; 1, 2 and 3 John; and Jude.

After discussing these last eight writings of the New Testament, the chapter will conclude with a summary and some final remarks. A short quiz on the book and a reading and prayer reflection will follow.

James

Background. Scholars are not absolutely sure who wrote this letter. Most think that James, the "brother of Jesus," is the author. This James may have been Jesus' cousin and the prominent leader of the Christian community in Jerusalem in the first decades of Christianity. He was martyred in the year 62, so if he was indeed the author of this epistle it may well have been written in the last few years of his life.

Or the author of this letter may have been writing under the pen name of James. This practice of attributing a book to another person certainly does not affect its divine inspiration. God reveals his word in the biblical writings whether or not we know who the author was.

In the New Testament times there were at least five kinds of biblical authorship. First, a person was considered the author if he wrote a book in his own hand. The gospel of Luke and the Acts are good examples of this kind of authorship. Second, authorship was attributed to a person who dictated a book to a scribe. Paul probably dictated most of his letters this way. Third, authorship was credited to a person who supplied the ideas for a book even though it was ghostwritten by someone else. Some people think that James may be an example of this kind of authorship. Fourth, a person was considered the author if the work was written by his disciples (even many years after the author's death) and reflected his words and teaching. 2 Peter and some of John's writings are probably examples of this kind of authorship. Finally, in a very broad sense, a person was considered the author if a work was written in the same kind of literary form for which he was famous. For example, the psalms are attributed to David though he certainly did not write all of them.

Catholic scholars suggest that 2 Peter and Matthew are probably works written by others and attributed to these famous men. More debatable examples are the Pastoral Letters, 1 Peter, Jude and James. If James was written under a pen name, it may have been written sometime in the 80s or 90s.

Occasion and themes of James. James was addressed to the "twelve tribes of the Dispersion" (Jas 1:1); that is, to Jewish Christians who lived somewhere outside of Palestine. It reads more like a written sermon or an instruction than like a formal letter; it does not have any clear outline. Basically the letter takes up two major issues. First, the author is very concerned about how wealthy Christians are treating the poor. The letter has some harsh things to say about money and the rich. At the same time it attempts to comfort poor Christians and assure them that God loves them in a special way.

The second concern is to correct an abuse which had crept into some Christian communities. Apparently some Christians thought that Paul's teaching on faith exempted them from doing good works. Paul, of course, had nothing of the sort in mind. When Paul wrote about the faith in Jesus that saves us—in his letter to the Romans for example—he made sure to include much practical advice on how to live the Christian life. James, too, stresses the relationship between faith and good works. Faith is not something abstract. Faith in the Lord must be reflected in good works of love for others. James gives many practical examples of what he means.

This letter, then, takes up practical concerns about Christian living. Though it was written for struggling Christian communities, it has much to teach us today.

Read James.

Then answer the following questions:

Chapter 1: What is the source of temptation?

OUR OWN WRONG DESIRES. 1:14

What is the point of vv. 19-27?

Practice the Word of GOD

Chapter 2: Why does class distinction have no place for Christians?

Love Thy Neighbor as Thyself

What makes faith true? Good WORKS 2:17

Chapter 3: What does the author have to say about the tongue?

3:6 Wicked Part of Body

Chapter 4: Which verse in this chapter defines sin?

4:4

Write that definition here:

anyone who chooses the world
for his Friend Turns himself into God's enemy.

Chapter 5: Why does James have such harsh words for the rich in this letter?

they condem the innocent 5:6
____

What sacrament is referred to in vv. 13-18? ________

Reconciliation
____

REFLECTION: Reread James 5:13-16. Do the following two reflection exercises.

1. How do you respond to these scriptural instructions? Answer yes (Y), no (N), or sometimes (S).

____ I talk over my problems with God when I'm in trouble.

____ When something good happens to me I thank and praise the Lord.

____ When I sin I make regular use of the sacrament of reconcilation.

____ When I'm sick I pray for the Lord's healing and ask my fellow Christians to pray for me.

____ In return, I pray for people who I know are sick.

2. *Who cares for you?* In the space provided, write the name of the person you would go to to talk about each of the following situations:

________________ I had a bad day at school and need to talk it out with someone.

________________ I am really sick and need some sympathy.

________________ I am ready to make an important decision about my future and need guidance.

________________ I need to borrow $20 for a date.

________________ I need to tell someone about something I did that was seriously wrong.

Discussion:

a. Why did you select the various persons you did? Would these people ever slander you? ("Slander"—spreading false statements about a person, in order to ruin his or her reputation.) What does James say about slander (see Jas 4:11-12)?

b. Comment: Love means standing with your friends when they are in trouble.

1 Peter

Background. It is hard for us today to imagine the sufferings of the early Christians. When they turned away from their pagan practices, their neighbors became highly suspicious of them. They no longer offered sacrifices to their various gods. They refused to go to the different worship services. They gave up certain sexual abuses which were widespread in the ancient world. In short, they began to live an entirely new life, a life based on the love of God and neighbor.

This changed life brought the Christians ridicule, verbal and physical abuse, persecution and suffering. Christianity and Christians where highly suspect. To accept Jesus Christ literally meant that one had to be willing to be torn apart by lions or wild dogs for him. Under the emperor Nero (A.D. 54-68) Christians were persecuted. You might recall that both Peter and Paul were probably martyred by him. The second great persecution took place toward the end of the reign of Domitian (A.D. 81-96) who insisted that everyone worship him as a god.

During these times of stress, persecution and suffering, Christian converts needed much encouragement from their spiritual leaders. 1 Peter is such a letter of encouragement. Probably authored by Peter toward the end of his life (A.D. 64-67), 1 Peter is written to the churches in Asia Minor. Many of the Christians in these churches were poor (1 Pt 2:18ff.); this letter tries to comfort and console them in the midst of their sufferings.

After the greeting in the first couple of verses, 1 Peter contains what appears to be an extended sermon on baptism (1:3-4:11). Geared to new converts, these chapters give important teaching on this sacrament and on what it means to be a follower of Jesus. Jesus' own life, especially as the Suffering Servant, is the prominent model of how Christians should live. Another major section of the epistle (4:12-5:14) gives specific advice and encouragement for Christians under persecution.

Read 1 Peter 1:1-4:11.

1. Find three indications in these chapters that this portion of the letter may have been directed to the newly baptized. Write the number of the verses here:

   a. ______________ b. ______________ c. ______________

2. What advice is given about the obligations of Christians toward

   a. pagans: ______________________________

   b. leaders: ______________________________

   c. masters (by their slaves): ______________________________

   d. husbands (by their wives): ______________________________

   e. wives (by their husbands): ______________________________

   f. each other: ______________________________

3. What is the meaning of 2:9-10?

   ____

4. Name one way Christians are supposed to imitate Jesus:

   ____

Read 1 Peter 4:12-5:14.

5. What attitude should Christians have in their sufferings?

   ____

6. Who wrote down Peter's letter? ______________________________

REFLECTION

A. For most people faith develops over a period of time. Right now you are probably seeking and questioning the meaning of your life and Jesus' role in it. Commitment to Jesus will vary from person to person. Suppose, for the sake of this exercise, that you firmly believe that Jesus is Lord. Suppose that you have decided to model your life on his. Modeling your life on Jesus means that you might have to be prepared to suffer because of your belief in him. Suffering for the Lord is a reality for many Christians in the world today. Imagine yourself in the following situations. What would you be most likely to do? Mark where you would be on the various continuums.

1. If the government took away my possessions because of my faith in Jesus, I would

   give up my faith ________________________ remain faithful

2. If I were imprisoned and tortured for Jesus, I would

   give up my faith ________________________ remain faithful

3. If I were forbidden to go to Catholic school, religion class or church, I would

   give up my faith ________________________ remain faithful

4. If I were not allowed to make a living and had to live in constant poverty, I would

   give up my faith ________________________ remain faithful

B. Rank yourself on each of these areas of spiritual advice given in 1 Peter. 1 is very low; 10 is very high.

a. *Example:* I give good example to those who are not of the same faith.

   1 2 3 4 5 6 7 8 9 10

b. *Authority:* I accept the authority of those over me: parents, teachers, government officials, etc.

   1 2 3 4 5 6 7 8 9 10

c. *Forgiveness:* I try to forgive anyone who hurts me.

   1 2 3 4 5 6 7 8 9 10

d. *Peace:* I am known as a peacemaker.

   1 2 3 4 5 6 7 8 9 10

e. *Suffering:* I cheerfully accept setbacks and offer them up to the Lord.

   1 2 3 4 5 6 7 8 9 10

Discuss:

1. Share your rankings with a friend.
2. How would you have rated yourself on these a year ago? If you've changed, to what do you attribute it?
3. Have you ever met a person who suffered for his or her faith in family or work life? Ask your parents to respond to this question.

1, 2 and 3 John

Background. From time to time in this book you have read about the philosophy of *gnosticism.* The gnostics believed that the physical world was inherently evil. They also believed that the body imprisoned the soul. To them, all life was a constant struggle between the cosmic forces of earthly darkness and heavenly light. Salvation came from secret knowledge (*gnosis* in the Greek) which was given to a select few by a bearer of light, a redeemer. The secret teaching of this lightbearer enabled the enlightened ones to escape the material world and obtain salvation.

The gnostics' false view of God's creation infected their views about Jesus. They taught, wrongly, that Jesus was the lightbearer, the savior, who taught secret knowledge only for the very intellectual to discover. Moreover, because the gnostics hated the material world, they taught that Jesus did not really have a physical body but only seemed to have one. This teaching itself had a name, *docetism,* which comes from the Greek word meaning "seem."

Christians who believed in gnosticism made three enormous errors: 1) They refused to believe that all of creation, including the human body, was good. This refusal goes against the Jewish and Christian revelation that all of created reality is good, in fact, very good (Gn 1:31); 2) They made Christianity a religion for the few. Jesus offered the good news to all, even the poor and ignorant. A person does not have to be a supreme intellectual to accept Jesus Christ. Even children can grasp Jesus' message of love and God's forgiveness, love and forgiveness meant for *all* people—not just the few; and 3) By rejecting the reality of Jesus' body, the gnostics rejected the incarnation of Jesus, his real death and his real resurrection. By denying these three key realities, the gnostics, in effect, rejected Christianity. If Jesus was not a human like us, then there is no guarantee that salvation has taken place. Salvation has been won through the life, death and resurrection of the God-*man,* Jesus Christ.

These gnostic ideas were circulating in the Christian churches in the last few decades of the first century; they became even more prominent in the second century. Each of John's letters warns against this heresy.

Authorship and date. As with John's gospel, we are not quite sure of the identity of the author of these three letters. He may have been John the Elder who is considered by some to be the final editor of John's gospel. Likewise, a precise date cannot be fixed for these three letters. The most common dates given are between 90 and 110.

1 John. The lengthiest of John's three letters is 1 John. It has often been called a commentary on John's gospel in that it reaffirms many of the key insights that can be found in the gospel. Above all else 1 John directly attacks the beliefs of the gnostics. Here are the major themes in 1 John:

1. *God's true revelation is found in faith in Jesus Christ.* There is not a new or higher revelation as the gnostics claimed, but only the Word of God who has existed since the beginning (1:1). God is righteous (2:29). God is love (4:8). God is life (5:20).

2. *To know God truly is to obey his commandments.* There is no secret knowledge involved in finding God. To know him means to follow the example of Jesus Christ and to obey his commandments (2:7-12). Jesus' human life is important because it is an example for us. If we don't follow Jesus' example we are not children of God (3:10). Christianity is not just right belief; it is also right practice.

3. *Love of God means love of others.* Gnosticism is exclusive in its love. Contrary to this, 1 John teaches:

   > Anyone who says, "I love God,"
   > and hates his brother,
   > is a liar (4:20).

   "God is love" (4:8) demands inclusive love of neighbor. Everyone is either our brother or our sister. The true Christian will not act superior to anyone and will not exclude anyone from his or her love.

2 John. Unlike 1 John which is a more general letter, 2 John is addressed to a particular church, "to the Lady, the chosen one, and to her children" (1:1). This short letter reaffirms the message of 1 John and warns the church to hold to the true doctrine about the incarnation of Jesus Christ (that he was God-made-man who dwelled with us). The author reminds his flock to love and expresses his wish to visit them very soon.

3 John. This letter may have been written before either 1 or 2 John. It is addressed to Gaius, a faithful disciple of John the Elder. He had been especially hospitable. The heart of this very brief letter is a condemnation of a certain Diotrephes (the head of the community) who seemed to be challenging John the Elder's authority. John expresses his wish to visit the church himself and settle the matter.

Both 2 and 3 John show that John the Elder held considerable authority over certain churches. In this regard he was similar to Paul.

Read and then summarize in your own words the following selections from 1 John:

Reading	*Summary*
1 John 1:8-2:2	______________________________
	______________________________
	______________________________
	______________________________
	______________________________
1 John 4:7-21	______________________________
	______________________________
	______________________________
	______________________________
	______________________________

REFLECTION

Here are some areas of life which often cause problems. Ask the Lord to help you with any that are a struggle for you.

- Drugs: "Everyone else is into them. Why not me?"
- Cheating: "You have to in order to get ahead."
- Lying: "Sometimes the situation demands it."
- Sex: "How far can I go?"
- Self-image: "I can't imagine anyone liking me."
- Language: "A few swear words now and then never hurt anyone."
- Conformity: "I don't like to stand out."
- Prayer: "There's no time."
- Money: "It's all I ever think about."
- Others: "Why should I go out of my way? They certainly don't for me."
- Parents: "They're always on my back."

Jude and 2 Peter

Authorship and date. These two letters are treated together because the author of 2 Peter borrows heavily from Jude's earlier letter. We do not know who the author of Jude was. He is identified with James as a "brother of the Lord" (probably a cousin). Verse 17 of the letter suggests that Jude was written for a second generation of Christians and verse 3 hints that Christian faith is an unchangeable deposit. These two references point to a late date for Jude's composition, perhaps sometime in the 80s.

There are many evidences in 2 Peter that someone other than Peter wrote this letter. It was written as late as 110-120. The author identifies himself with Peter to show that his intention is to give teaching that goes back to apostolic times.

Content of the letters. Like John's letters, the epistle of Jude is concerned with gnostic influence. Jude writes against the belief that moral conduct is not that important to one who has been saved by Jesus. Jude corrects the false belief that what one does in one's body has little effect on his or her spiritual life. This false belief was a favorite theme of the gnostics. It justified much sinful behavior.

2 Peter uses much of Jude in its second chapter. This letter also reaffirms the teaching of Jesus' second coming. Perhaps by the time this letter was written—and it seems to be the last work composed in the New Testament—people did not pay that much attention to the doctrine of the *Parousia,* the doctrine of Jesus' second coming. 2 Peter reminds his readers that the Parousia will come. It also teaches the divine Lordship of Jesus and insists on actions that befit a Christian life.

Revelation

The Bible's last book is its most difficult to understand. Scripture scholar William Barclay cites an ancient scholar who said that the study of the book of Revelation either finds a man mad or makes him mad. St. Jerome commented that it contains as many secrets as it does words.

The highly symbolic language of Revelation has prompted many people throughout the ages to treat it as an allegory with hidden meaning for each age to discover. Many of these same people have applied Revelation to their own current historical situation. Even today there are popular books that pretend to use Revelation to predict the exact hour of the end of the world. These books point to natural disasters like earthquakes and tornadoes, to dictators like Hitler, to wars and threats of wars as sure signs that we are living in the last age. Forgetting that Jesus warned against such speculation, these books frighten their readers with the message of Christ's immediate return. Some people, as a result, leave their jobs, flee to the wilderness or countryside and with great expectation await the end of the world.

This kind of predicting the future is misreading Revelation. To guard against misapplication of this work, two important points must be kept in mind at all times: 1) the exact nature of the kind of writing that appears in Revelation—apocalyptic writing; and 2) the historical setting in which Revelation was written.

1. *Apocalyptic writing.* Revelation is also known as Apocalypse. *Apocalypse* means "to reveal" or "to unveil" the mystery of God. Apocalyptic writing was a very common form in Jewish circles from 200 years before Christ to 200 years after Christ. The book of Daniel from the Old Testament (especially Dn 7-12) is one of the prominent examples of this kind of writing; Revelation borrows heavily from it and other Old Testament apocalypses.

Apocalypses were written in times of great crisis. As a form of literature they spoke about the end of history and the coming of God's kingdom, the New Age. The chief purpose of this kind of writing, especially in times of great persecution and suffering, was to keep alive hope and trust in God and to remind people that God is in final control of history—not the evil rulers of this world. Apocalyptic writings, through the use of symbols, stressed that the New Age—a golden age of God's peace and justice—is God's gift. He is in control of the events. Nothing that men and women do can usher it in.

2. *Historical context of the book of Revelation.* Much light is shed on the meaning of Revelation by paying attention to the times in which it was written. Most scholars date the book around A.D. 95. At that time the emperor Domitian was insisting on emperor worship. He claimed divinity. In fact, he insisted that his subjects burn incense yearly at an altar built to him and proclaim him God, "Caesar is Lord." The penalty for refusal was death.

No true, faithful Christian would ever worship Caesar. Many were put to death for their belief that only Jesus Christ is Lord. A prophet by the name of John, perhaps a disciple of the apostle John, was exiled to the island of Patmos because he preached the gospel. He wrote Revelation primarily to reassure persecuted Christians that God would ultimately triumph. In elaborate poetic language, John records a number of visions which tell of the defeat of evil—personified by the Roman Empire—and the ultimate triumph of the Lord. Revelation promises that those who endure to the end and remain faithful to Christ will reign with him at the end of time.

Why symbolic language? Why did John write an apocalypse to convey this rather straightforward message of endurance in the time of persecution? One of the most plausible reasons is that John could then write about the Roman persecutors by the use of symbols. In the time of crisis in which Revelation was written, John could console and encourage his fellow believers freely without his book being totally suspect. By using symbols he could convey what he was talking about clearly to his readers without the Romans ever discovering that they were the object of the writing.

Some of the symbols in Revelation deal with Christ. He is the Lamb with seven eyes (which depict his universal knowledge) and seven horns (which symbolize his universal power). Numbers themselves are symbols. "7" means wholeness or perfection; "6" means imperfection; "4" represents the whole world (the four corners of the earth); "12" refers to Israel or the apostles; "1000" means immensity or eternity; and so forth.

Rome is described as Babylon, the ancient persecutor of the Jews. She is called a prostitute, and anyone who worships the emperor is accused of fornication or adultery. The two emperors who persecuted Christians are also given symbols. Nero and Domitian are both called beasts. Evil, personified by Satan, is a dragon. War and persecution are brought by the "four horses of the Apocalypse."

Colors also are given symbolic meanings. Each of the visions of the prophet is loaded with symbols.

Of course we should never take any of this literally. The meaning we are to get from Revelation is that we must be faithful to

Christ, even in time of persecution. God is ultimately in control. One day, through Christ, God will totally destroy all the evil forces in the world. As a matter of fact, that day has already come. In heaven, the battle is won and God alone is worshipped. There is no evil. There is peace and justice. There is unutterable joy. Christians who remain faithful to Christ must never forget that he alone is King of kings. All of history will soon be under his peaceful reign.

Outline of Revelation. No one can agree on a suitable outline of Revelation. One popular outline arranges the book into seven parts of seven; another arranges the book into six series of six. Rather than a detailed outline, here are several key themes from Revelation:

1. *Prologue* (chapter 1): How John wrote the book.
2. *Letters to the seven churches* (chapters 2-3): Advice to seven churches in Asia Minor ("seven" means that these churches represent the whole church) who are encouraged to remain true to Christ in the midst of their persecutions.
3. *John's vision of God* (chapters 4-5).
4. *Visions of the day of the Lord:*
   a. *Seven seals (chapters 6-7): disasters*
   b. *Seven trumpets (chapters 8-11): terror*
   c. *Serpent (chapters 12-14): his beasts war on the earth*
   d. *Seven bowls (chapters 15-16): plague*
   e. *Babylon (chapters 17:1-19:10): the harlot Rome, her defeat and rejoicing in heaven.*
5. *Final defeat of the beast and the 1,000-year reign* (chapters 19:11-20:6)
6. *Final conflict* (chapter 20:7-15): Satan is cast into hell; a general resurrection and final judgment.
7. *New Jerusalem* (chapters 21-22): A new heaven and a new earth established.

To read Revelation with understanding takes much time and patience. A commentary is a useful tool to help one grasp this difficult book. But to get some idea of what is in Revelation, sample the following chapters. Answer the questions below each suggested reading.

Read 1:1-3:22 Letters to the seven churches.

Prologue: 1:1-3

Does it appear from these opening verses that John was looking *far* into the future?

____________________ Why or why not? __________

____

Address and greeting: 1:4-8

List three titles John gives to Jesus in this section:

a. ____________________________________

b. ____________________________________

c. ____________________________________

Alpha (A) is the first letter of the Greek alphabet; omega (Ω) is the last letter. What does John mean when he calls Jesus "the Alpha and the Omega"?

____

Beginning of the vision: 1:9-20

What does John have in common with the recipients of his letters?

____

Who is the Son of Man? ____________________ He is described in symbolic language. What does this language say about him?

____

The seven letters: 2-3

These churches were all in the same region, connected by the same ancient road. List one fault and something John praises in each of them.

Ephesus ____________________

____

____

Smyrna ____________________

____

____

Pergamum ____________________

____

____

Thyatira ____________________

____

____

Sardis ____________________

____

____

Philadelphia ____________________

____

____

Laodicea ____________________

____

____

If you number these churches 1 through 7, do the odd or even numbers seem to get the most praise?

____

Might this be symbolic? ____________________

Read 12:1-13:8 Dragon and beasts.

The woman may represent Israel or perhaps Mary. The dragon represents the devil who is, of course, evil. The devil works through two beasts: Domitian and Nero. The number 666 represents ultimate imperfection because it falls short of the perfect number 7 three times. Many scholars believe it refers to Nero. In the Greek and Hebrew languages, each letter is assigned a numerical value. (You are probably familiar with Roman numerals where I is 1, V is 5, X is 10, etc.) The name Caesar Nero, written in Hebrew letters and given the numerical equivalent for each letter, adds up to 666.

Who does the woman bring into the world?

____

How do we know that this is who the person might be?

____

Can the dragon defeat God?

____

What blasphemous title may have been written on the coronet (13:1)?

____

What does the second beast probably want God's people to do?

____

Read 19:11-21: First battle of the end.

What is the outcome of the battle? ____________________

What does this outcome mean? ____________________

Read 21:1-22:5: The New Jerusalem.

What is being described here? ____________________

Why is there no need for a temple in the new city?

____

What *feeling* would this passage give to Christians who were being persecuted for their faith?

____

SUMMARY

1. The writings of James; 1 and 2 Peter; 1, 2 and 3 John; and Jude are known as the Catholic Epistles because they are directed to the universal or general church.

2. Some of the biblical writings were written under a pen name whereby a book was attributed to some other author, usually from apostolic times.

3. James criticizes the wealthy and stresses that faith in Jesus demands that one perform good works for others.

4. 1 Peter comforts Christians undergoing persecution. This letter teaches many baptismal themes and aims at bolstering the faith of relatively new converts.

5. 1 John reaffirms the theology of John's gospel and attacks gnostics who were questioning the true humanity of Jesus. It contains beautiful passages on the meaning of love. 2 John also attacks gnosticism, while 3 John is concerned with a problem of church leadership.

6. 2 Peter borrows heavily from the short letter to Jude. Both of these letters are concerned with the wrong behavior of gnostics. 2 Peter also teaches about the second coming of Jesus, the Parousia.

7. Revelation is a difficult work to understand. Loaded with symbolism, Revelation is a type of literature known as *apocalyptic;* it treats the coming of the New Age, the gift of God's heavenly kingdom. Revelation must be understood in its historical context, a period when Christians were being put to death for not worshipping the emperor Domitian. Its important message is that God will ultimately triumph over evil and that the patient suffering of Christians will be rewarded in heaven.

SOME FINAL REMARKS

You have made it to the end of this textbook. Congratulations! The text has introduced you to the most powerful book you will ever read: the good news about Jesus Christ. You have read a great number of passages from the New Testament. Perhaps in your study you have learned a great deal more about Jesus our Lord—and about yourself.

The message of these 27 books of the New Testament is very simple. The following four points will help summarize what the New Testament is saying:

- Our God is a loving Father who made the universe, including us. He is intimately concerned with our welfare and wishes to share his life with us.

- Men and women have stubbornly resisted the invitation of God's love. We need to be saved from our sinfulness and our rejection of our loving Father.

- God so loved us that he sent his only Son, Jesus, to us. Jesus sacrificed for us by dying on the cross. He showed us how to live through a life of incredible generosity, sensitivity and concern. He overcame death and sin through his resurrection. He offers us his life even now. We can have his friendship now. We can meet him right now: through prayer; in the sacraments, especially the Eucharist; in small groups gathered in his name; through reading his word; in each other; in the least of our brothers and sisters. This is incredibly good news which demands a response on our part. We are invited to accept Jesus Christ and then live a life of love in imitation of him.

- The Father and the Son give us the gift of their love, the Holy Spirit. It is the Holy Spirit who enables us to recognize that Jesus is the Lord. He empowers us to call God "Abba." He strengthens us to live as Jesus did. He binds us into a community of love, the church. Moreover, he draws us into the union of love which is the life of the Trinity—Father, Son and Spirit.

Where do you go from here? The reading of the Bible is essential for Christians, even young Christians. It contains the key to our life in Christ. It is God's word. What can you do now that you have completed this course? Here are some ideas:

- Resolve to read the New Testament for 10-15 minutes each day. You now have the tools to help your reading. You may wish to try the following:

    1) Study an individual New Testament book with the help of a good commentary.

    2) Study a New Testament theme by reading all the passages which treat it. A concordance would help you locate all the places where a theme is mentioned. Here are some examples: kingdom of God, faith, love, friendship, salvation, forgiveness.

    3) Study New Testament passages at random. Biblical commentaries and dictionaries can help you study them in depth.

- Pray for 10-15 minutes each day using the New Testament. Select a favorite passage as an introduction to your prayer. Read it as though the Lord is speaking directly to you. Picture the Lord calling you by name. Then, listen to what he is saying. If you do this, your life will change dramatically.

- Form a scripture study group at school or in your parish. Meet on a weekly basis. Study a book of the Bible together. Perhaps a concerned teacher, parish priest or adult friend will help you get started.

Short Quiz on the Book

You have learned a lot of material about the New Testament. Check to see how much of it you remember. The pages where the correct answers can be found are given at the end of the quiz. Your teacher can also help you find correct answers if you need help. Good luck.

Circle the correct answer or fill in the blank:

1. Which form of speech was most characteristic of Jesus' own teaching? a. apocalyptic b. parables c. epistolary d. liturgical e. none of these

2. The theology contained in the two infancy narratives is identical. (True or False)

   Which two gospels record these infancy narratives?

   a. ______________________ b. ______________________

3. The history of Paul's three missionary journeys is found in

   ____

4. The theme of a journey to and from Jerusalem dominates the theology of which New Testament writer? a. Matthew b. Luke c. John d. Paul e. the author of the pastoral epistles

5. A common source for both John's and Matthew's gospels was a. Luke's gospel b. *Q* c. an ancient passion narrative d. no common tradition

6. Perhaps the most famous collection of Jesus' moral teaching is

   ____

   which is found in ______________________________ gospel.

7. Which title of Jesus definitively asserts his divinity?
a. Servant of God b. Son of Man c. Christ d. Lord
e. Son of David

8. Writing under a pen name means that a New Testament work is not inspired. (True or False)

9. Which is the most important miracle in John's gospel?

____

10. The resurrection story contains eyewitness accounts of the actual raising of Jesus. (True or False)

11. This writer is responsible for one-fourth of the New Testament and is considered by most people to be its best writer. Who is he?
a. Luke b. John c. Paul d. can't be determined

12. John's gospel highlights which of the following themes:
a. Jesus is light of the world b. Jesus is God's Word
c. truth vs. untruth d. all of these

13. If you did not understand the meaning of the biblical word *Parousia,* where would be the best place to go for help?
a. the book of Revelation b. a bible dictionary c. a concordance d. a synopsis e. a biblical atlas

14. Which gospel seems to be most concerned with the proper identity of Jesus as Messiah? a. Matthew b. Mark c. Luke
d. John

15. Mark, Matthew and Luke are called the ______________ gospels because they can be "read together."

16. The major theme of Paul's greatest letter, Romans, is
a. We will participate in the resurrection of Jesus.
b. Jesus is the head of his body, the church.
c. Following Jesus demands joyful suffering.
d. Salvation is a free gift of God that demands faith.

17. The latest New Testament work written is a. 2 Peter
b. 3 John c. Jude d. Revelation

18. Write from memory five of the seven last words of Jesus:

a. ____________________

b. ____________________

c. ____________________

d. ____________________

e. ____________________

19. In a brief paragraph summarize what you think the New Testament is saying:

____

____

____

____

____

____

20. Which of the following is not considered one of the "great" letters of Paul? a. 1 Corinthians b. Galatians c. 2 Corinthians d. Colossians

21. The proper way to read the book of Revelation is to find the meaning of its many symbols for our own history. (True or False)

22. The three stages in the growth of the New Testament are

a. ____________________

b. ____________________

c. ____________________

23. Redaction criticism is a. concerned with the editorial work done on a certain work b. concerned with the small units of material which make up the final product c. concerned with the historical Jesus d. concerned with the meaning of the text of a work for Christians today

24. Which of the following groups did not believe in a resurrection from the dead? a. Pharisees b. Essenes c. Sadducees d. Zealots

25. An especially dangerous philosophy to early Christian belief was a. Stoicism b. Epicureanism c. Gnosticism d. cult of Osiris

CORRECT ANSWERS to this quiz can be found on the following pages of the text:

1. pp. 149-151
2. pp. 109-112
3. p. 197
4. pp. 138-139
5. pp. 79, 174
6. pp. 118-121
7. p. 125
8. p. 227-228
9. pp. 181-182
10. p. 158
11. pp. 130-134
12. pp. 168-169
13. pp. 38-39
14. pp. 86-88
15. p. 79
16. pp. 212-213
17. p. 237
18. pp. 93-95
19. p. 246
20. pp. 215-217
21. p. 239
22. p. 14
23. p. 33-34
24. p. 61
25. pp. 233-234

Final Reading and Prayer Reflection

Read prayerfully and reflectively this beautiful hymn that Paul wrote to the Ephesians (Eph 1:1-14). Then, using all the tools at hand and the knowledge you have gained in this course, carefully analyze the passage. Answer the questions in the right-hand column.

From Paul, appointed by God to be an apostle
of Christ Jesus, to the saints who are faithful
to Christ Jesus: Grace and peace to you from
God our Father and from the Lord Jesus Christ.

—what is meant by "apostle"?
—who are the "saints"?

Blessed be God the Father of our Lord Jesus Christ,
who has blessed us with all the spiritual
blessings of heaven in Christ.

—what does "blessed" mean?
—what is the significance of the title "Lord"?

Before the world was made, he chose us, chose
us in Christ,
to be holy and spotless, and to live through
love in his presence,
determining that we should become his adopted
sons, through Jesus Christ
for his own kind purposes,
to make us praise the glory of his grace,
his free gift to us in the Beloved,
in whom, through his blood, we gain our freedom,
the forgiveness of our sins.

—what does "adopted sons" mean?
—why were we chosen?
—"his blood" refers to what?
—what does "freedom" mean here?

Such is the richness of the grace
which he has showered on us
in all wisdom and insight.

He has let us know the mystery of his purpose,
the hidden plan he so kindly made in Christ from
the beginning
to act upon when the times had run their course
to the end:
that he would bring everything together under
Christ, as head,
everything in the heavens and everything on earth.

—what does "mystery" mean?
—what does this mean?

And it is in him that we were claimed as
God's own
chosen from the beginning,
under the predetermined plan of the one who
guides all things
as he decides by his own will;
chosen to be,
for his greater glory,
the people who would put their hopes in Christ
before he came.

—who does "we" refer to?
—does this mean we have no freedom?
—what does "glory" mean?
—who are the "people"?

Now you too, in him,
have heard the message of the truth and the good
news of your salvation,
and have believed it;
and you too have been stamped with the seal of
the Holy Spirit of the Promise,
the pledge of our inheritance
which brings freedom for those whom God has taken
for his own
to make his glory praised.

—who does "you" refer to?
—how have we heard?
—what does this mean?
—when did it happen?